The Fundamentals
of
Argument Analysis

*Essays on Logic as
the Art of Reasoning Well*

Richard L. Epstein

Advanced Reasoning Forum

For more information contact:
Advanced Reasoning Forum
P. O. Box 635
Socorro, NM 87801 USA
www.ARFbooks.org

paperback ISBN 978-1-938421-05-1
e-book ISBN 978-1-938421-06-8

The Fundamentals of Argument Analysis

Essays on Logic as the Art of Reasoning Well

Richard L. Epstein

There is no end but only a continual beginning.

Essays on Logic as the Art of Reasoning Well

Dedicated to

William S. "Bill" Robinson

with much gratitude for his criticisms,
encouragement, and friendship for many years

Preface

This series of books presents the fundamentals of logic in a style accessible to both students and scholars. The text of each essay presents a story, the main line of development of the ideas, while the notes and appendices place the research within a larger scholarly context. The essays overlap, forming a unified analysis of logic as the art of reasoning well. In order that they may be read independently there is some repetition among them.

The question addressed in this volume is how we can justify our beliefs through reasoning.

The first essay, "Arguments," investigates what it is that we call true or false and how we reason toward truths through arguments. A general theory of argument analysis is set out on the basis of what we can assume about those with whom we reason. This essay serves as background for all the succeeding ones.

The next essay, "Fallacies," explains how the classification of an argument as a fallacy can be used within that general approach to argument analysis. In contrast, there is no agreement on what the terms "induction" and "deduction" mean, and, as discussed in "Induction and Deduction," they are not useful in evaluating arguments.

In reasoning to truths we must take some claims as basic, not requiring any justification for accepting them. How we choose those and how they affect our reasoning is examined in "Base Claims."

The essay "Analogies" considers how comparisons can be used as the basis for arguments, arguing from similar situations to similar conclusions. An important use of analogies is in reasoning about the mental life of other people and things, which is studied in "Subjective Claims," written with Fred Kroon and William S. Robinson.

"Generalizing" examines how to argue from a part of a collection or mass to the whole or a larger part. The large question there is whether we are ever justified in accepting such an argument as good.

"Probabilities" sets out the three main ways probability statements have been interpreted: the logical relation view, the frequency view, and the subjective degree of belief view. Each of those is shown to be inadequate to make precise the scale of plausibility of claims and the scale of the likelihood of a possibility.

Many discussions of how to reason well and what constitutes good reason are given in terms of who or what is rational. In the final essay, "Rationality," it's shown that what we mean by the idea of someone being rational is of very little use in evaluating reasoning or actions.

I hope in this book to give a clearer idea of how to reason well, setting out methods of evaluation that are motivated in terms of our abilities and interests. At the ground of our reasoning, though, are metaphysical assumptions, too basic and too much needed in our reasoning for us to try to reason to them. But we can try to uncover those metaphysical assumptions to see how they are important and what depends on them, as I do throughout this volume.

Acknowledgments

Many people have helped me over the nearly twenty years I have been working on this material, and I fear that I cannot recall all whom I should thank. But William S. Robinson and Fred Kroon have given much of their time and thought to suggestions that have improved all these essays; much of the discussion of rationality and emotions comes directly from conversations with Fred Kroon. They and the other members of the Advanced Reasoning Forum have helped me to understand the issues here. I am most grateful I to all of these. The mistakes, however, remain mine.

Publishing history of the essays in this volume

This is the first publication of "Subjective Claims" and "Base Claims."

"Rationality" was the keynote address of the first meeting of the Advanced Reasoning Forum in 1999. It was first published as an appendix to my *Five Ways of Saying "Therefore"*. A discussion of the notion of rationality for actions has been added, and the notes have been expanded to include comparisons to more views of rationality.

The other essays are revisions of work that first appeared in either my *Critical Thinking* or *Five Ways of Saying "Therefore"*.

Arguments

We reason as a means to many ends. One of those is to arrive at truths. This we do with arguments. Here we'll see what an argument is, set out criteria for what counts as a good argument, and then look at how to evaluate those conditions.

Claims

We use speech to communicate and to reason with each other. So it is speech we will focus on here.

Claims A claim is a written or uttered piece of language that we agree to view as being either true or false.

In what follows, I'll use *utterance* for both written or uttered parts of speech, including silent talk to ourselves.

We don't have to make a judgment about whether a part of speech is true or is false in order to classify it as a claim. We need only judge that in the context in which it's uttered it's reasonable to assume that it is one or the other. A claim need not be an *assertion*: a piece of language put forward as true by someone.

The word "agree" suggests that it is a matter of convention whether we take a sentence to be a claim. But almost all our conventions, agreements, assumptions are implicit. Our agreements may be due to many different reasons or causes, compatible with many different assumptions about the nature of the world.

We normally identify utterances that look or sound the same, as when Dick says "Ralph is not a dog," and later when Suzy is convinced she says, "I agree. Ralph is not a dog," taking that to be the same claim he made. This does not require that we believe in abstract objects like types of sentences, but only that we have some method of identifying distinct utterances as equivalent for our purposes in reasoning.

These points are discussed more fully in "Truth and Reasoning" in *Prescriptive Reasoning*. Here I'll try to clarify them with examples.

Example 1   Dogs are mammals.

  Analysis   This is a claim, one we recognize as true.

Example 2   Two apples together with two more apples are five apples.

  Analysis   This is a claim, one we recognize as false.

Example 3   Zoe: Dick is upset.

  Analysis   Zoe said this in a whisper to Tom when she and Dick were visiting him. Tom might not know whether it's true or false, but he knows it's one or the other.

Example 4   Zoe (to Dick, while she's pointing): Look! Crows.

  Analysis   In this context Dick takes Zoe's exclamation "Crows" to be a claim. It's true or false, for it could be crows or it could be blackbirds she's pointing to. A claim need not be a sentence.

Example 5   Zoe: What did you think of Wanda's dancing?
    Dick: Pee yew.

  Analysis   We all understand Dick to mean that he thinks Wanda's dancing was "stinky," that is, very bad. We're justified in viewing the utterance as a claim. Speech can include not only regular parts of spoken languages, but also parts of signed languages, as well as gestures and interjections, though we'll focus here on ordinary language speech, and in particular sentences.[1]

Example 6 I wish I could get a job.

Analysis If Maria, who's been trying to get a job for three weeks, says this to herself late at night, then this isn't a claim. It's more like a prayer or an extended sigh.

But if Dick's parents are berating him for not getting a job, he might say, "It's not that I'm not trying. I wish I could get a job." That might be true, or it might be false, so the example would be a claim.

It is not a sentence type or an inscription devoid of context that is a claim. A claim is a specific piece of language in a specific context.

Example 7 $2 + 2 = 4$

Analysis Some say that this sentence is a claim and no context is necessary for us to know that. But that's highly debatable, as I explain in "Mathematics as the Art of Abstraction" in *Reasoning in Science and Mathematics* in this series of books.

Example 8 Dick (to Suzy): How can anyone be so dumb as to think that cats can reason?

Analysis We might think that Dick is asserting that cats can't reason. But that's not what he said. Without some further context we're not justified in viewing this as a claim.

Example 9 Zoe (to Dick): Shut the door.

Analysis A command is not true or false, so regardless of the context, this is not a claim.

Example 10 The United States is a free country.

Analysis This is too vague to classify as a claim, at least in any context in which what we mean by "free country" is not made explicit.

Example 11 Dick: My Lit professor showed up late for class today.
Zoe: What do you mean by late? 5 minutes? 30 seconds? How do you determine when she showed up? When she walked through the door? At exactly what point? When her nose crossed the threshold?

Analysis   This is just silly. Zoe knows "what he meant," and the sentence isn't too vague for her to agree that it is true or false. The issue isn't whether a sentence or piece of language is vague, but whether it's *too vague*, given the context, for us to be justified in saying it is true or false.

Example 12   Wanda is fat.

   Analysis   Wanda weighs 120 kgs and is 1.7 m tall, so almost all of us would agree with this example. We take it to be a claim.

   If Wanda weighed only 50 kgs, we'd all disagree with it, which shows that then we'd take it to be a claim, too.

   But if she weighed 72 kgs, we'd be unsure. It isn't that we don't know what "fat" means, we just don't think the sentence is true of false. We don't classify it as a claim. It isn't that our notion of claim is vague: we're clear that we won't classify it as true or false. It's the sentence itself that is too vague in that context to classify as a claim.

   But if there's no clear division between what we mean by someone being fat or not being fat, doesn't that mean that we don't have a clear notion of claim? No. That we cannot draw a line does not mean that there's no obvious difference in the extremes.

Drawing the line fallacy   It's bad reasoning to argue that if you can't make the difference precise, then there's no difference.

Inferences
Often we don't know whether a claim is true or whether it's false, but we want to investigate what follows from it or whether it follows from some other claims.

Inferences   An *inference* is a collection of claims, one of which is designated the **conclusion** and the others the **premises**, which is intended by the person who sets it out either to show that the conclusion follows from the premises or to investigate whether that is the case.

Example 13   Tom: Ralph is a dog. All dogs bark. So Ralph barks.

   Analysis   This is an inference with premises "Ralph is a dog" and "All dogs bark" and conclusion "Ralph barks." The word "so" is not part of the inference; it is used to indicate that the claims are meant to be taken as an inference and that "Ralph barks" is the conclusion.

Example 14   Flo: Ralph is a dog. All dogs barks. So probably Ralph barks.

Analysis   This is an inference with the same premises and conclusion as the last example. The word "probably" indicates Flo's attitude toward the conclusion; it is not part of the conclusion itself.

Indicator words   An *indicator word* is a word that is used to indicate the role of a claim in an inference or the speaker's attitude about whether the claim is true or false. It is not part of the inference.

Example 15   You may own stocks or securities which are selling at a lower price than when purchased. Tax considerations might call for a sale of such securities in order to produce a currently deductible tax loss. However, if it is desired to still own the securities while producing a tax loss, you can't just sell securities at a loss and then buy them right back. Any purchase of the same securities within 30 days before or after the sale negates any losses. To get around this restriction, you can purchase similar but not identical securities to the ones sold. Or, in the case of bonds, you can achieve the same result by making a swap through a brokerage house.   *Tax Guide for College Teachers*, 1994

Analysis   This collection of claims is not an inference, for there is no intent to show that one of them follows from one or more of the rest.

There are various uses of inferences in reasoning: arguments, explanations, mathematical proofs, conditional inferences, and causal inferences are examined in this series of books. What counts as a good inference depends on which kind we're evaluating. Here we'll look at arguments.

Arguments

Arguments   An *argument* is an inference that is intended by the person who sets it out to convince someone, possibly himself or herself, that the conclusion is true.

An argument is not an abstract thing; it is a linguistic utterance used for a purpose. The premises of an argument are asserted as leading to, or supporting, or establishing that the conclusion is true.

In classifying a collection of claims as an argument we must take into account (what we think is) the intent of the speaker.[2]

Example 16   Lee (to Suzy): Ralph is not a dog. I've seen him. He's a puppet.

   Analysis   Lee is trying to convince Suzy that "Ralph is not a dog" is true. He uses as evidence for that the claims "I (Lee) have seen him" and "He (Ralph) is a puppet." These constitute an inference, though there's no indicator word. We interpret Lee's intent in making these utterances.

Example 17   Dick (to Harry): Sheep are the dumbest animals. If the one in front walks off a cliff, all the rest will follow. And if they get rolled over on their backs, they can't right themselves.

   Analysis   Dick is trying to convince Harry that "Sheep are the dumbest animals" is true. He's given two reasons, that is, premises, for believing that.[3]

Example 18   Dick (to a policeman): I'm telling you I'm not at fault. How could I be? She hit me from the rear. Anytime you get rear-ended it's not your fault.

   Analysis   Dick is trying to convince the policeman that "I'm not at fault" is true. He uses two claims as premises which he thinks show that the claim is true.

Example 19   Zoe's mother (to Zoe): How come you don't call me? What's wrong? You don't love your mother? Where did I go wrong?

   Analysis   Zoe's mother is trying to convince Zoe, but she's not trying to convince her that a particular claim is true. She's trying to convince Zoe to call her. This is not an argument.

Example 20   Suzy (to Zoe): How can you go to the movies with Wanda and not me? Don't you remember how I took care of Spot when you and Dick were gone?

   Analysis   It seems that Suzy is trying to convince Zoe that "You should go to the movies with me instead of Wanda" is true by using the premise "I took care of Spot when you and Dick were gone." But before we begin interpreting questions as claims we should have a clearer idea of how to evaluate arguments.

What counts as a good argument? It's not that the argument succeeds in convincing, for an argument that Dick gives to Tom and Suzy that cats are dangerous is not bad because Tom's sleepy and can't follow it and Suzy loves cats too much to accept its conclusion. Though arguments are meant to convince, we need criteria we can use to evaluate them that do not depend wholly on how a particular person responds to it.[4] We take as our basic criterion the following.

Good argument An argument is good if it gives good reason to believe that its conclusion is true.

The rest of this essay, indeed the rest of this book will be concerned with trying to make clear what we mean by good reason to believe a claim.

Plausible claims

If an argument is to give us good reason to believe its conclusion we should have good reason to believe its premises, for from a false claim we can as easily reason to a false conclusion as a true one. Consider:

The Prime Minister of England is a dog. All dogs have fur.
So the Prime Minister of England has fur.
(false premise, false conclusion)

The Prime Minister of England is a dog. All dogs have a liver.
So the Prime Minister of England has a liver.
(false premise, true conclusion)

Example 21 Tom: Almost all wombats bark. So the new wombat at the zoo barks.
Dick: "Almost all wombats bark"? Why should I believe that?
Analysis Tom's argument would certainly give Dick good reason to believe the conclusion if Dick had good reason to believe the premise. But he hasn't, and he responds by asking for just that.

For an argument to be good, we have to have good reason to believe its premises. But we also need to recognize that we have good reason to believe them and actually believe them. These are distinct conditions.

Example 22 Dick (to Suzy) Cats are the most dangerous common pet.
Suzy: I don't believe that.

Analysis Dick has good reason to believe this claim: he's read about all the diseases that cats can give people, including, it's now suspected, schizophrenia. He sets out to convince Suzy. He presents all the evidence he has. He comes back again the next day and gives her more evidence, all from authoritative sources. He reminds her of people she knows who are ill from cat allergies. She accepts all that yet she still says, "I don't believe it." We may say she is irrational, but nonetheless we can't deny that it's possible to have good reason to believe a claim, recognize that you do, and still not believe it.

Example 23 Tom: People who are poor just don't want to work hard.

   Analysis Tom has no good reason to believe this claim, yet he believes it.

Example 24 The earth is not flat.

   Analysis Dick believes this and reckons he has good reason to believe it: he's seen pictures of the earth taken from satellites, and he trusts the sources of those. He didn't have good reason to believe it when he was five years old.

   Harry believes this and has good reason to believe it because he's seen reasoning that leads to it in his physics course.

   Suzy has good reason to believe the claim because she's heard people say it and she trusts them as authorities, as indeed they are. And she believes it.

   A woman living in a stone age culture in the Amazon basin of Brazil who never considered the claim before has no good reason to believe it, and might not believe it.

Plausible claims   A claim is *plausible* to a particular person at a particular time if:
   • The person has good reason to believe it.
   • The person recognizes that he or she has good reason to believe it.
   • The person believes it.

   Plausibility is not an either-or classification. We have an informal scale for each of the conditions, from better reason to believe to worse reason to believe, from recognizing clearly to being oblivious, from believing strongly to strongly disbelieving. Combined, we have an informal scale from the least plausible to the most implausible.

Example 25

   a. All dogs bark.

   b. A meteor larger than 1,000 km in diameter will hit the earth by the end of next week.

   c. It will not freeze in July in New York City next year.

   d. No human can survive for more than two hours with body temperature above 113 degrees Fahrenheit (45 degrees Celsius).

   e. Two apples plus two more apples are four apples.

Analysis We know that (a) is false: Basenjis can't bark, and some dogs have had their vocal cords cut. We rate it the lowest on the scale of plausibility. Claim (b) is implausible, too, since we suspect that any meteor of that size would be spotted by astronomers were it that close to earth, and we would have heard about it. Claim (c) seems more plausible, but it could freeze in New York in July even though it never has in recorded history and all we know about weather suggests it won't, at least in our lifetime. Claim (d) seems very plausible, though not certain. And claim (e) is clearly true.

Can we can make this scale of plausibility more precise?

We can say that each claim in this list is more plausible than the preceding one. But what we cannot seem to do, except for the first and last, is assign numbers to these claims from 0 for clearly false to 1 for clearly true that accurately reflect our judgments. Is claim (c) plausible to degree 0.7? Or 0.8? Is claim (d) plausible to degree 0.98 or only 0.91? Any assignment of numbers as measures of the plausibility of these claims seems arbitrary, though perhaps useful as markers to remind us of our comparative judgments.

Example 26 Compare:

   Most dogs bark.

   Most dogs are pets.

Analysis Though both of these are plausible, there doesn't seem to be any way to decide which is more plausible. Though we can compare the plausibility of many claims, it seems highly unlikely that we can compare the plausibility of any two claims. This and the last example suggest that we cannot replace the informal scale of plausibility with a precise mathematical one based on a theory of probability, as I discuss further in "Probabilities" in this volume.

Though we do not have precise measures of plausibility, we can often compare the plausibility of claims and by being explicit about our background we can usually agree on whether we accept them as plausible. If we did not think that we can share our judgments of what is plausible, we would have no motive for trying to reason together. In what follows, if I say a claim is *plausible* without specifying a particular person, I mean it's plausible to most of us now, as I'm writing: we have good reason to believe it, we recognize that we have good reason to believe it, and we do believe it. A claim is *implausible* or *dubious* if it is not plausible.

Contrary claims and suspending judgment

Example 27   Almost all dogs bark.

Analysis   This is plausible to most of us. Dick in particular finds it plausible. So he knows he doesn't have good reason to believe "Almost all dogs don't bark" because that and the example can't both be true, though both could be false.

Contrary and contradictory claims   Two claims are *contrary* if it's not possible for both of them to be true at the same time in the same way. Two claims are *contradictory* if any way the one could be true the other is false.

Note that contradictory claims are also contrary.

Example 28   Dick: Wow! Your cat Puff is definitely not healthy.
Suzy: No, he's healthy.
Dick: (*pointing to Puff*) You call that healthy?
Tom: I think both of you are right.

Analysis   Tom finds both "Puff is healthy" and "Puff is not healthy" plausible. But that's because he reckons both of those are vague enough to talk that way. That's the only way he can accept "Puff is healthy and Puff is not healthy" as true, at least if he's using "not" in the way we usually do.

Absolutely fundamental to our reasoning is the idea that no claim is both true and false. If we don't accept that, then we have no filter, no way to distinguish good reasoning from bad.[5] Let's amend our definition of claim to make this explicit.

Claims   A claim is a written or uttered piece of language that we agree to view as being either true or false *but not both*.

If we were to have good reason to believe both a claim and a contrary of it, we'd have good reason to believe both that the claim is true and that it's false. Whatever we mean by "good reason to believe a claim," it can't include that.

Good reason and contrary claims   If someone has good reason to believe a claim, then he or she does not have good reason to believe a contrary of it.

Suspending judgment   If someone does not have substantially better reason to believe a claim than to believe a contrary of it, then he or she does not have good reason to believe either of them. In that case he or she should suspend judgment on whether the claim is true.

These are prescriptive principles, circumscribing what we accept as good reason to believe a claim and what counts as a good argument. They don't rule out that people do believe contraries even when they recognize they're contraries. But they tell us that if they do, and if they accept an argument as good that has a premise that is contrary to one they find plausible, then they are not reasoning well.

Example 29   No medieval book on logic is known to have been written by a woman.

Analysis   You probably have no reason to believe this. But you probably have no reason to believe "Some medieval book on logic is known to have been written by a woman." In that case, you have good reason to suspend judgment on whether the example is true or whether it is false.

Example 30   Harry: I've read what the economists and financiers have been saying, and it seems to me there's good reason to believe that the economy will recover from the current recession and start growing at more than 3% in the next twelve months. But looking at what the politicians are doing, and reading these other economists, it seems to me that there's good reason to believe that the economy won't grow at all through the next two years.

Analysis Harry seems to have good reason to believe both a claim and its contrary. But he knows he can't have good reason to believe them both. So he should suspend judgment.

Begging the question

Plausible premises are necessary for an argument to be good. But that's not enough.

Example 31 Suzy: God exists.

Harry: That's just superstition.

Suzy: But the Bible says so.

Harry: Why do you think that's true?

Suzy: Because God wrote the Bible.

Analysis Suzy is trying to convince Harry that "God exists" is true. But she takes as premise "God wrote the Bible," which is less plausible to Harry than "God exists." So her argument gives Harry no better reason to believe "God exists" than he had before he heard it.

Example 32 Suzy: Dr. E is mean.

Wanda: Why do you say that?

Suzy: Because he's not nice.

Analysis Suzy is trying to convince Wanda that "Dr. E is mean." But "Dr. E is not nice" is not more plausible to Wanda than "Dr. E is mean." Any reason she has to believe the one is already reason to believe the other. So Suzy's argument can't give her more reason to believe "Dr. E is mean" than she had without the argument.

Example 33 Maria (to Lee): Every dog has a soul, so you should treat dogs humanely.

Analysis The conclusion is plausible to Lee. He finds the premise plausible, too. But it's not more plausible to him than the conclusion. So Maria's argument gives him no more reason to believe the conclusion than he had before he heard her argument.

Begging the question   An argument *begs the question* if it has a premise that is not more plausible than its conclusion.[6]

Example 34 Most dogs are pets. Virtually all dogs that are pets bark. So most dogs bark.

Analysis Earlier we couldn't see how to compare the plausibility of "Most dogs are pets" and "Most dogs bark." Unless we can resolve that and say that the former is more plausible than the latter, we're not justified in accepting this argument as good.

Example 35 Tom: Maria is a widow.
Lee: So Maria was married.

Analysis The argument "Maria is a widow, so Maria was married" would seem to beg the question, since we would normally say that "Maria is a widow" is less plausible than "Maria was married." But the reason Lee has to believe "Maria is a widow" is because Tom told him, and he knows that Tom is a good friend of Maria, and he trusts Tom. So he concludes, "Maria was married," which he didn't have reason to believe before. Until he concluded it, it wasn't plausible to him. The argument in this context isn't begging the question.

Whether an argument begs the question depends on context. But that shouldn't be surprising, for whether a claim is plausible depends on context, and indeed whether an argument is good depends on context.

For an argument to be good the premises have to be plausible and more plausible than the conclusion. But that's not enough.

The conclusion follows from the premises

Example 36 Dollar bills are printed using green ink. Therefore, U.S. currency is easy to counterfeit.

Analysis Our reaction to the single true premise here is "So?" Why does "U.S. currency is easy to counterfeit" follow from that? When we ask "So?" we're asking why the conclusion follows from the premises.

For an argument to be good, the conclusion should follow from the premises. In this essay we'll set out the basic issues about what we mean by this, which we'll examine more in the remaining essays.

Valid inferences

Valid inferences An inference is *valid* if it is impossible for the premises to be true and conclusion false at the same time and in the same way.

If an inference is valid, then certainly the conclusion follows from the premises: there's no way it could be false if the premises are true. Since arguments are inferences, they, too, are classified as valid or invalid.

Example 37   All dogs bark. Ralph is a dog. Therefore, Ralph barks.

Analysis   This is a valid inference. But viewed as an argument it's bad because we know that the first premise is false.

valid argument ≠ good argument

Example 38   Richard L. Epstein is the author of this essay. So Richard L. Epstein is bald.

Analysis   This is invalid: I could be young and have a full head of hair. But I don't, so doesn't that show there is no such possibility? In evaluating an inference for validity we are consider what is possible, not just what is actually the case.

This last example suggests that we must reject determinism to analyze arguments. Even though I'm bald, I could have had a full head of hair. But that's just one way to think about possibilities.

To invoke a way the world could be in evaluating an inference, that is, to discuss a possibility, we have no choice but to use a description. Some consider possibilities to be abstract, but for our purposes it's enough to consider descriptions, for it's through those that possibilities enter into our evaluating reasoning. A description is a collection of claims: we suppose that this, and that, and this might all be true at the same time. We do not require that we give a complete description of the world, for no one is capable of presenting such a description nor understanding one if presented.

What qualifies some collections of claims as describing a possibility and others not? We require that a description of a way the world could be must at least be consistent. That is, it cannot have or entail a contradiction; it must be *logically possible*. So there is no possibility in which there is a square circle. But there seems to be no contradiction in postulating that a dog could give birth to a donkey: it is logically possible.

By using collections of claims to stand in for possibilities or as descriptions of possibilities, we need not commit ourselves to a possibility being something real, such as a world in which I'm not bald.

A determinist can say that invoking possibilities is just a way to factor into our reasoning our ignorance of how the world is.

The criteria for when a collection of claims constitutes a description of a way the world could be, which is how I'll loosely put it, can sometimes be given an objective standard relative to particular view of the nature of the world codified in a formal logic, as I discuss in "Valid Inferences" in *Reasoning and Formal Logic*. But often the best we have is a willingness to agree, perhaps until we are shown wrong, that à particular collection of claims is indeed a description of a way the world could be.

Example 39 All dogs bark. Spot is a dog. So Spot barks.

Analysis This is valid. Yes, the first premise is false. But it could be true: some evil person could eliminate all dogs that don't bark. In that case were the second premise also true, the conclusion would be true, too.

Example 40 Richard L. Epstein is the author of this essay. All essay authors are women. So Richard L. Epstein is a woman.

Analysis The conclusion is false. But the inference is valid: there is no way the premises could be true and conclusion false. To describe the world as being such that I am a man is not such a possibility, for that contradicts the premises.

Example 41 Every mammal has a kidney. So every dog has a kidney.

Analysis This is invalid. It could be that there is some dog with no kidney.

But every dog is a mammal. Doesn't that make such a description of the world impossible? No, for that is to talk about what is the case. If we add as a premise "Every dog is a mammal," then the inference indeed would be valid.

What we take into account of our knowledge of the world in evaluating an inference as valid is what we have stated as the premises of the argument, nothing more. Possibilities are relative to just those claims.

If an inference is valid, then the conclusion follows from the premises, for if the premises actually are true, then the conclusion is true, too. But only rarely do we have occasion to use a valid argument.[7]

Strong arguments

Example 42   Dick heard this morning that there are parakeets for sale at the mall. He knows that his neighbor has a birdcage in her garage, and he wonders if it will be big enough for one of those parakeets. He reasons:

> All parakeets anyone I know has ever seen or heard or read
> about are under 50 cm tall.
> Therefore, the parakeets on sale at the mall are under 50 cm tall.

Analysis   Dick thinks that, yes, a new supergrow bird food could have been formulated and the parakeets at the local mall are 1 meter tall, he just hasn't heard about it. Or a rare giant parakeet from the Amazon forest could have been discovered and brought here for sale. Or a UFO might have abducted a parakeet, hit it with growing rays, and it's now gigantic. All of these ways the premise could be true and conclusion false are highly unlikely to Dick. So he reckons he has good reason to believe the conclusion, even though the argument is not valid.

Example 43   Tom (to Wanda): Dick is a bachelor. So Dick was never married.

Analysis   Wanda knows that Dick is a bachelor. But this argument gives her no reason to believe he was never married, for she knows that lots of men who are bachelors were married before. The conclusion does not follow from the premises.

Strong and weak inferences   An inference is *strong* if it is possible but unlikely for the premises to be true and conclusion false at the same time and in the same way; it is *weak* if it is neither valid nor strong.

Only invalid inferences are classified as strong or weak. Invalid arguments, being inferences, are strong or weak, too.

Example 44   John F. Kennedy was President of the United States. Therefore, John F. Kennedy was Japanese.

Analysis   We know that the premise is true and conclusion false. So the argument is clearly not strong.

Example 45   All swans anyone has ever seen or heard of are white. Therefore, all swans are white.

Analysis This argument was strong when made in the 1500's in Europe, where it was understood that "anyone" meant anyone in the world of which they knew. And there was good reason to believe that the premise was true, as indeed it was, and better reason to believe the premise than the conclusion.

The argument is not good now. But that is not because it's not strong. It is still unlikely that the premise could be true and conclusion false at the same time. The argument hasn't gone from strong to weak. Rather, the premise is known to be false: Europeans have seen black swans in Australia.

John Stuart Mill in discussing this argument suggests that for a strong argument to be good it must have a true conclusion:

> That all swans are white, cannot have been a good induction, since the conclusion has turned out erroneous.[8]

But the issue isn't whether the conclusion is false, it's whether we happen to know it is false.

The strength of an inference is not an either-or classification. We have a scale from the weakest to the strongest as we deem the possibilities we consider in which the premises are true and conclusion false to be more or less likely. Arguments that lie in the broad center of the scale and the clearly weak ones are certainly not good. We needn't bother to classify arguments as bad versus very bad, since any bad argument tells us nothing about the conclusion we didn't already know.

Example 46 Compare:

a. Almost all dogs bark.
   Spot is a dog.
   So Spot barks.

b. Almost all dogs bark.
   Spot is a dog.
   Spot is not a basenji.
   So Spot barks.

c. Almost all dogs bark.
   Spot is a dog.
   Spot is not a basenji.
   Spot has not had his vocal cords cut.
   So Spot barks.

d. Almost all pets that bark are dogs.
   Spot is a pet and barks.
   So Spot is a dog.

e. Almost all pets that bark are dogs.
   Spot is a pet and barks.
   So Spot is not a dog.

Analysis Argument (b) is stronger than argument (a) because the additional premise has eliminated some of the ways we considered earlier in which the premises of (a) could be true and conclusion false. Argument (c) is stronger than argument (b) because it has eliminated further possibilities. Exactly where we place (a) on the scale is not precise, and any attempt to put a number to it seems arbitrary. But there is nothing arbitrary about our evaluation of argument (b) as stronger than (a), and (c) as stronger than (b).

We can also compare arguments (d) and (e): since (d) is strong, (e) is weak.

But which of (a) and (d) is stronger, we cannot say. We can't compare how many dogs there are that don't bark to how many pets there are that bark and aren't dogs. We're asking whether the conclusion follows from the premises, and for that we need to consider possible ways the premises could be true. There is no reason to think we can compare the strength of any two arguments. There is no reason to believe that for every argument we can or theoretically could assign a number to the likelihood of its conclusion being true given that the premises are true.

It would be wrong to conclude from these observations that because we cannot make the notion of the strength of an argument precise, the notion is worthless. That would be a drawing the line fallacy.

Can a strong argument be good? To answer that we need to understand better the strong-weak scale of arguments.

Evaluating the likelihood of a possibility
In the context of judging an argument as strong or weak, what do we mean when we say that a possibility is unlikely?

Example 47 (again) Dick is a bachelor. So Dick was never married.

Analysis When we classified this as weak, we said it was not unlikely that Dick could have been married. Any claim that rules out "Dick was married" is not plausible, or at least not more plausible than the conclusion, "Dick was never married," unless perhaps you know more about Dick than is stated in the premise.

Example 48 Maria's hair is naturally black. Today Maria's hair is red. So Maria dyed her hair.

Analysis Could the premises be true and conclusion false? Yes: Maria might be taking a new medication that has a strong side effect, or she might have gotten too close when they were painting her car. But we can rule out those possibilities with plausible claims: "There is no medication that causes people's hair to turn from black to red," "People standing close to a car getting painted who get paint on them get it on more than their hair." We ponder and can think of no possibility in which the premises are true and conclusion false that we can't rule out with a plausible claim. Perhaps there is one, but since we can't come up with one, we deem the argument strong.

Example 49 (again) All parakeets anyone I know has ever seen, or heard, or read about are under 50 cm tall. Therefore, the parakeets on sale at the mall are under 50 cm tall.

Analysis The possibilities we considered in Example 42 are unlikely, for we can rule them out with plausible claims such as "No one has discovered a 1 meter tall parakeet in the Amazon and brought it back to the mall for sale," "Aliens did not abduct a parakeet," "There is no supergrow bird food that makes parakeets grow 1 meter tall." Dick can't come up with any other possibilities for the premises to be true and conclusion false that he can't easily rule out with plausible claims, so the argument is strong for him.

Our evaluation of the strength of an argument is relative to what we believe: "likely" means "likely to us." Typically, though, the scale from strong to weak is not so completely relative to a particular person that there is no hope we can agree on the strength of arguments. Suppose we disagree. I find a particular argument strong, and you find it weak. If we wish to reason together, you should describe to me a way the premises could be true and conclusion false that you think is not unlikely. That may depend on knowledge you have of how the premises could be true which I do not have, but once you've made that explicit we can agree or disagree that there is such a possibility. The only issue, then, would be whether we agree that the possibility is likely. Sometimes we can't agree on a determination, but further examination will leave us with a clearer understanding of what our differences in evaluation are based on more than just whim. When the beliefs involved in determining the strength of an argument are made explicit, determining the argument to be strong or weak is far more likely to be a shared judgment. This is the same observation we made about the plausibility of claims, and it must be, since the strength of an argument can be reduced to consideration of the plausibility of claims describing possible ways the world could be.

But we don't always come to an agreement. How can we proceed to evaluate an argument in the absence of a shared judgment?

Example 50   Wanda: Spot is a dog. I know 'cause Tom told me. So Spot barks.

Zeke: Why? Spot could have had his vocal cords cut to stop his barking. Or Spot could be a basenji, a type of dog that doesn't bark. Or Spot could have had his bark bitten out of him by a coyote.

Wanda: That's just silly. Those possibilities are really unlikely.

Zeke: They don't seem silly to me.

Wanda: Well, show me they're likely.

Analysis   Wanda believes her argument is strong; she doesn't accept that the possibilities Zeke offers are likely. Zeke disagrees and says that the argument is weak. Who's right?

Wanda is trying to convince Zeke, and possibly herself, that "Spot barks" is true. Zeke does not say that "Spot barks" is false. He only gives some reason to think the argument isn't strong, so he can suspend judgment. But is he suspending judgment unreasonably? Is it just that he can't recognize a strong argument when he's given one?

Wanda says that each of "Spot had his vocal cords cut," "Spot is a basenji," and "Spot had his bark bitten out of him by a coyote" are unlikely. If that's so, then she should be willing to add one or more premises that rule out those possibilities: "Almost no dogs have had their vocal cords cut," "Very few dogs are basenjis," "Next to no dogs have had their bark bitten out of them by a coyote." With those added, the argument is strong. Then the evaluation of the argument rests on whether those claims are plausible.

An argument is not strong by default   If someone offers a description of the way the world could be in which the premises are true and conclusion false, then the burden is on the person who claims that the argument is strong to show that the possibility is unlikely by adding a premise that is plausible which shows that such a possibility is unlikely.

This does not relieve the person who objects to the evaluation of an argument as strong from making clear his or her reasons for thinking that a possibility is likely in order to try to come to some shared evaluation of the strength of the argument. Only in those cases where sharing our background knowledge does not resolve our differences do we have to appeal to this principle. That can happen in reasoning about much more substantial issues with real disagreements about our background, as you can see in "Subjective Claims" in this volume (pp. 120–123).

Taking account of what we (think we) know

The judgment that an argument is strong is always provisional, for it depends on what we know about the world and what we have considered in our evaluation.

Example 51 At most 1.13% of all pigs on this farm have swine flu. Therefore, it is extremely likely that hog number 87318 does not have swine flu.

Analysis The words "it is extremely likely that" are not part of the conclusion: they are the speaker's evaluation of the strength of the relation between the premises and the conclusion, which is "Hog number 87318 does not have swine flu."

Here it seems we have an objective standard for evaluating the strength of this argument: there is at most a 1.13% chance that the premise could be true and conclusion false. So the argument is strong. But that's only if we know nothing more about hog number 87318 than that it lives on this farm. If we saw it in front of us sniffling and moaning, we'd be right to evaluate the argument as weak, for we'd have reason to believe "Hog number 87318 is sniffling and moaning" as well as "Hogs that sniffle and moan are sick."

Example 52 When I was living in Cedar City, Utah someone in New Zealand heard these two arguments:

a. In Cedar City, Utah over 90% of the population is Mormon. Richard L. Epstein lives in Cedar City, Utah. So Richard L. Epstein is Mormon.

b. At least 90% of all people with the name "Epstein" are not Mormon. So Richard L. Epstein is not Mormon.

Analysis The premises of both these arguments were plausible to that person and more plausible than the conclusion. Each was clearly strong. So each gave good reason for him to believe its conclusion. So if a strong argument is good, he had good reason to believe both "Richard L. Epstein is Mormon" and "Richard L. Epstein is not Mormon." Something is wrong.

The problem arises from considering the two arguments separately. Once we accept that the premise of (b) is plausible, (a) is no longer strong; similarly if we deem the premise of (a) to be plausible, (b) is no longer strong. For either argument to be strong we need to assume something more:

> Nothing else is known about Richard L. Epstein that would distinguish him from all other people living in Cedar City as regards whether he is Mormon.

For a strong argument there is always a possibility that the premises could be true and conclusion false. If we happen to know that such a possibility is actually so, or if we have good reason to believe that such a possibility is the case, then we should not say it is unlikely that the premises could be true and conclusion false. Our evaluation of an argument as strong is relative to what we have good reason to believe.

But no one can survey all that he or she believes is true. Even if we could do a reasonably close job of that, none of us is going to do it regularly every time we reason. Rather, as with much else in our reasoning, the classification depends not only on what we know but what we're paying attention to. Our judgments about arguments can be corrected as we find out or are reminded of more information than we originally took into account.[9]

Example 53 There are one million lottery tickets. One ticket is drawn. No one has seen what it is. Therefore, it is not ticket number 1.

Analysis This is strong, with plausible premises that are more plausible than the conclusion. But if this is a good argument, so is the same reading "2" for "1." And so is the same reading "3" for "1." . . . And so is the same reading "1,000,000" for "1." Thus, it seems, we have good reason to believe each of those one million conclusions. So consider the following argument with one million and one premises:

> There are one million lottery tickets.
> Ticket number 1 was not drawn.
> Ticket number 2 was not drawn.

⋮

Ticket number 617,261 was not drawn.

⋮

Ticket number 1,000,000 was not drawn.

Therefore, no ticket was drawn.

This argument is valid and, if the reasoning above was correct, we have good reason to believe each of the premises. That gives us good reason to believe the conclusion. But the conclusion is clearly false. This is the *lottery paradox*.

The confusion here is that though we may have good reason to believe any one of the premises, we do not have good reason to believe all of them together. Once we have concluded that we have good reason to believe "It is not ticket number 1" is true, the argument that shows we have good reason to believe "It is not ticket number 2" is weaker; not a lot weaker, but weaker than if we hadn't believed the conclusion for "1," since we can rule out at least one possibility. Once we accept the conclusion of the argument for each of "1," "2," . . . , "617,260" not being drawn, the argument that "617,261 was not drawn" is weak. We do not have good reason to believe each of the one million conclusions unless we forget that we have good reason to believe the others.

Can we make explicit in our arguments this reliance on taking account of what we know in determining whether an argument is strong? Consider arguments of the form:

(1) Q of the collection A is B.

 a is A.

So a is B.

Even when Q is a sufficiently high percentage or a quantifier such as "almost all" or "nearly every one" we do not automatically have a strong argument, as Examples 51 and 52 show. We need something more:

(2) Nothing else is known about a that would distinguish it from everything else in A as regards whether a is B.

Perhaps we could add (2) to arguments like (1), along with a claim that (2) is sufficient to give us good reason to believe the conclusion, and then have a valid argument. But compare the following:

(3) Almost all dogs bark.
     Juney is a dog.
     (4) Juney is not a basenji.
     So Juney barks.

Argument (3) is a stronger and better argument than the same argument without (4), since (4) rules out lots of possibilities. A claim like (2) does not strengthen an argument by ruling out possibilities. Rather, (2) is part of our method of evaluating whether an argument is strong. This is clearer if we try to formulate a general claim that would work for every argument that we intend to judge for its strength.

(5) We have no reason to believe it is likely that the premises could be true and conclusion false.

This is part of how we define "strong argument." It is not another premise we can add to the argument without falling into an infinite regress. We cannot "improve" a strong argument by adding a premise about our knowledge.

Converting strong arguments into valid ones?

We might hope to avoid relying on strong arguments in our reasoning by converting every argument that is intended to be judged for its strength into an argument that can be judged for validity.

     Consider:

     Almost all dogs bark.
     Spot is a dog.
     So Spot barks.

This is a strong argument, which, if a strong argument can be good, is good. But the first premise, it is often said, is too vague. We should replace the argument with a precise mathematical version:

     98.236% of all dogs bark.
     Spot is a dog.
     So there is a 98.236% chance that Spot barks.

Invoking the mathematics of probability and statistics, the argument can be judged as valid or invalid.

     But how do we get such a statistical premise? After all, we use the vague "almost all" when we don't know an exact number. Typically it is through some strong argument that we arrive at a belief in such a statistical claim. If so, then we have substituted a valid argument for a strong one but only by relying on a further strong argument.

If we were to deal with all apparently strong arguments in this manner, then we should replace the conclusion of (a) in Example 52 with "There is a 90% chance that Richard L. Epstein is Mormon," and the conclusion of (b) there with "There is a 90% chance that Richard L. Epstein is not Mormon." But no mathematical analysis can resolve from these now valid arguments which, if either, of the original conclusions we have good reason to believe.

Moreover, though converting some claims into statistical ones makes good sense, as in "The chance that the die will show 1 when it is thrown is 1/6," in other cases it is a confusion, as in "Probably Dick is over 1.85 m tall." Either Dick is over 1.85 m tall or he isn't; "probably" is not part of the claim but a comment on our belief about "Dick is over 1.85 m feet tall".

Statistical analyses play two different roles in arguments. They can be the subject matter of an argument, and hence a statistical claim can be a conclusion. Or they can be part of how we decide how strong an argument is. The latter cannot be incorporated into the argument. Turning strong arguments into statistical ones that should be judged for validity does not resolve whether an argument gives us good reason to believe its conclusion.

Certainty

Still, someone might say we should not rely on strong arguments because they give us no certainty. Though we might have good reason to believe the conclusion of a strong argument, we cannot be certain of it, as we can with a valid argument.

But an argument gives no more reason to believe its conclusion than we have for believing its least plausible premise. If the premises of a valid argument are not obviously true, then the argument gives us no reason to think the conclusion is certain.

Example 54   No dog hibernates. Juney is a dog. So Juney does not hibernate.

Analysis   This is a valid argument. The first premise of it is plausible. If challenged as to why we believe it, the best we can do is invoke something like the following argument:

(a) No dog anyone has ever seen or heard of hibernates.
     Biological theory suggests that it it is not possible for
         a dog to hibernate.
     Therefore, no dog hibernates.

We do not have to add (a) to the example, for the example as it
stands is good. We have good reason to believe the first premise,
which, if pressed, we can elaborate. Still, it's enough we have good
reason. But we are not absolutely certain that "No dog hibernates" is
true, nor do I see how we could be.

We have a division of what might be good arguments relative to
whether they yield certainty:

   i.   Valid arguments that yield certain conclusions because
        their premises are certain.

   ii. Valid arguments that yield uncertain conclusions because
        their premises are uncertain.

   iii. Strong arguments that yield uncertain conclusions because
        their conclusions are only very probably true relative to
        their premises.

The difference between arguments of type (ii) and (iii) is not that an
argument of one has a conclusion of which we can be certain and the
other doesn't, but why the conclusion is uncertain. The conclusion of
a valid argument is as certain as its least plausible premise, whereas
the conclusion of a strong argument may be less certain than its least
plausible premise. As with the last example, often the difference is
where we allow uncertainty to enter into our reasoning: in the premises
or in the move from the premises to the conclusion.

For category (i) we have a further division:

   a. Valid arguments that we can determine are valid.
   b. Valid arguments that we are not sure are valid.

The latter may yield uncertain conclusions because we may be
uncertain that the argument is valid.

If we should accept only what we can justify with certainty, we
will be able to use only valid arguments that we can recognize are valid
and which have premises we know with certainty. There are such
arguments: I feel cold, therefore, I don't feel hot. Not many, but some.

Indeed, so few that if we restrict ourselves to only valid arguments with certain premises, we will have little scope for reasoning in our lives.

Example 55 Anubis is a dog or Anubis is a coyote.
>If Anubis is a dog, then Anubis barks.
>If Anubis is a coyote, then Anubis howls and yips.
>So Anubis barks or Anubis howls and yips.

Analysis Even though Lee has had some practice in reasoning, he doesn't recognize this argument as valid. Does that make the argument bad? We want to say no, the problem is that he can't reason very well.

In evaluating arguments we assume that the other person is knowledgeable about the subject, so we can come to some agreement about the evaluation of the plausibility of premises and, in the case of evaluating invalid arguments, the likelihood of possibilities. We also assume that the other person can reason well. These assumptions are what justify us in saying "The argument is good even if you don't recognize that it's good." The assumption that someone can reason well is not sharp. Much more complicated valid arguments could be given, and we have no clear line where we should say you ought to be able to recognize these as valid.[10]

We do not have this problem with strong arguments. For an argument to be strong, it must be clear to us that it is strong. Part of what it is to be a strong argument is that we judge as unlikely any possibility in which the premises are true and conclusion false.

Can a strong argument be good?

We've seen that a strong argument with premises that are plausible and more plausible than its conclusion gives us some reason to believe its conclusion. But does it gives us good reason to believe its conclusion?

The answer may in part be determined by our metaphysics and what particular notion of truth we have adopted. The platonist might say no. All reasoning with strong arguments is too tainted by experience to be reliable.

But even an empiricist might say no. We can only refute general principles, not prove them. All we can justify with our reasoning are statistical generalizations based on valid mathematical principles, mathematics being allowed into the canon of the empiricist's methods.

If strong arguments are not acceptable, then there will be little scope for reasoning in our ordinary lives. Some will concede this and say that a strong argument can give us some reason to believe its conclusion is true, but not good reason. We can have good reason to believe a conclusion only if the argument is valid. In most of our reasoning we'll have at best likelihoods, and we should be satisfied with that.

This, it seems to me, is part of a view that only certainty, which is usually coupled with objectivity, is acceptable in reasoning well. Strong arguments may be useful in our daily lives, though not useful for gaining real knowledge or belief. But just as with the dichotomy of the true and false, we have the dichotomy of what we will act on as if it were true, or as the best bet, and what we won't. Unless paralyzed by a confused skepticism, we will in many cases in our lives need to act on conclusions of strong arguments.[11]

I am content to study how we can come to some pretty good if not perfect reason to believe claims, since that's what you and I need in our lives. I will leave to others the study of perfect reason to believe, logic not as the art of reasoning well for us but for the gods. If strong arguments are not in the canon of good reasoning, they are certainly in the canon of pretty good reasoning.[12]

Good arguments

We now have three conditions for an argument to be (pretty) good for a particular person at a particular time:

- The premises are plausible to that person at that time.
- Each premise is more plausible to that person than the conclusion.
- The person recognizes that the argument is valid or strong.

An argument does not give good reason to believe a claim in some general, abstract way. It gives a particular person at a particular time good reason to believe its conclusion. It would seem, then, that we cannot have a notion of a good argument but only of a good argument for you then, or me now, or her last week. But in practice, as a community we have a stock of claims that most of us find plausible. Some may disagree with us, and in trying to explain why we can often find a deeper understanding of our assumptions about the world. But as a rule we can and do make judgments about whether we have good reason to believe a claim that are generally accepted by our community. Similarly, we can generally agree about how likely a possibility is in evaluating whether an argument is strong. If this were not the case we could not use arguments to advance our knowledge but only to advance my knowledge or your knowledge. We would have little motive to write arguments for others to read. The notion of what counts as a good argument need not be relative to each particular person but can be and is relative to our community. So even if an argument is not good for this person, it can nonetheless be classified as good for most people.

Conditions for an argument to be good

- The premises are plausible.
- Each premise is more plausible than the conclusion.
- The argument is valid or strong.

We've seen that each of these conditions is independent of the other two. We've also seen why these conditions are necessary. In practice they are taken as sufficient. We'll consider whether they should be sufficient in the rest of the essays in this volume. We'll start by considering how to repair apparently defective arguments.

Repairing Arguments

Sometimes it's obvious that an argument is good. But more typically we are presented with arguments that are lacking.

Example 56   Lee: Tom wants to get a dog.
  Maria: What kind?
  Lee: A dachshund. And that's really stupid, since he wants one that will catch a Frisbee.

Analysis   Lee has given an argument:

Premises: Tom wants to get a dog that will catch a Frisbee.
Conclusion: Tom would be stupid to get a dachshund.

Someone who doesn't know what a dachshund is would think this is a weak argument. But we know that Lee has just left out what's obvious to most of us: Dachshunds are too low to the ground, they can't run fast, they can't jump, and the Frisbee is bigger than they are, so they couldn't bring it back. Any dog like that is a bad choice for a Frisbee partner.

Should we classify Lee's argument as bad? Or should we say that it's just lacking obvious premises which when supplied make it good?

When are we justified in supplying a premise? If we have no general method, no rules for when we can repair arguments, we will classify bad arguments as good or repair every argument we encounter into one that is to our liking without regard to what the person making the argument intended. We will not respect the other person's reasoning, nor we will learn from the arguments we encounter.

A principle of charity
The most common analyses of why and how we should repair arguments invoke a principle of charity:[13]

> In general, the Principle of Charity says this: When analyzing reasoning always analyze it in the way that interprets it as the strongest possible reasoning compatible with the inference indicators in the discourse.
>
> The Principle of Charity makes sense not only in terms of kindness and perhaps, fairness, to authors (because we do not attribute bad reasoning to them unless they are clearly guilty of it), but also in terms of our own personal self-interest. Speaking at least for myself, my aim in studying logic is not so much to refute other people's arguments as it is to find the truth through reasoning.
> —Stephen Naylor Thomas[14]

> PC: When reconstructing an argument, try to formulate a reconstruction that is well-formed, has reasonable premises, and is undefeated. In other words, make the argument as strong as possible.
>
> We should adhere to (PC) not because it is nice to do so or because people who give arguments need or deserve charity, but because adhering to (PC) leads us to consider the best available arguments and thus to gain the most insight into the issue we are analyzing. —Richard Feldman[15]

> When more than one interpretation of an argument is possible, the argument should be interpreted so that the premises provide the strongest support for the conclusion.
> —Jerry Cederblom and David W. Paulsen[16]

> In reconstructing an argument into standard form, one should supply any missing parts, if they are implicitly present. The so-called *Principle of Charity* requires that an opponent's argument always be formulated in its strongest possible version. This includes supplying any missing elements—but only those that are regarded as part of the original intention of the arguer. —T. Edward Damer[17]

There are two problems with adopting a principle along these lines. First, we have no justification for adopting it. Of course we want to learn and understand, but why should we adopt this principle towards that end? Why should we always make the strongest possible argument? What is assumed about the person making the argument?[18]

Second, adopting this principle will lead us to interpret almost every argument as good, since "as strong as possible" must mean (except in the last quote) as good an argument as we can make. No guide is offered for distinguishing when an argument is bad and when it is incomplete. In extreme form this leads to the position that there are no mistakes in reasoning, just misinterpretations of others' intentions in arguing.

Here is an example of how these problems arise in practice, from an anonymous review of a draft of my textbook *Critical Thinking*.

> I would have to disagree with the author that there is no premise that could be added to the argument:
>
>> Dr. Epstein gives fair exams.
>> Great teachers give fair exams.
>> So, Dr. Epstein is a great teacher.
>
> so as to make it a good argument. The author writes, "We can't know what those premises might be." Rather, I think we might add these:
>
>> Besides giving fair exams, Epstein exhibits all the other qualities which contribute to making a teacher great.
>> And anyone who exhibits all those qualities is a great teacher.
>
> One could, I think, yet object to certain details about these premises, but there is no doubt that, if added to the premises of the argument above, they result in an argument which is arguably good.

This is wrong. The original argument is bad, having the form: all A are B, b is B, so b is A. That is not only invalid, here it is weak. There is no reason to assume that the person making the original argument believes "Epstein exhibits all the other qualities which contribute to making a teacher great." I know no one who exhibits all those qualities, whatever they may be. Nor is there justification for someone to add weaker premises, say, "Epstein lectures well," or "Epstein organizes his courses well," since he does not know if those are true or whether the person making the argument believes them. We don't know how to make this into a better argument. Yet a principle of charity enjoins us to make it as strong as possible.

Maurice Finocchiaro also wishes to be charitable. He suggests we are often wrong in calling an affirmation of the consequent a fallacy.

> Someone who says "If P then Q; Q; therefore P" could be construed as saying "Q; the fact that P would explain the fact that Q; therefore, no other explanation of Q being available, we may presume P."
>
> To show that the actual argument is a fallacy, the logician has to argue that it is deductive.[19]

This is wrong on two counts. First, there is a clear and reasonable presumption that anyone who is affirming the consequent without saying more is confusing it with an application of *modus ponens* or confusing "if" with "only if." Second, the type of reasoning Finocchiaro describes, inference to the best explanation, is also a mistake in reasoning.[20]

Finocchiaro is right to stress that arguments that are not bad are often mistakenly classified as fallacies. But that does not mean that the good reasoner has the obligation to make every defective argument good. Lots of people argue badly lots of the time, and they recognize they are doing so when it's pointed out to them.

Taking a principle of charity as the foundation of argument analysis gives us no clear method. There is no reason to think that different people will agree on how to repair an argument using such a vague guide.

The Principle of Rational Discussion

To classify a collection of claims as an argument we need to assume that the speaker (or writer) is attempting to convince someone that a particular claim is true based on the truth of other claims. Thus, fundamental to any theory of argument analysis are the intention and capabilities of the person who is making the argument. What of those intention and capabilities should we take into account?

The Principle of Rational Discussion   We assume that the person with whom we are deliberating or whose argument we are reading:

    a. Knows about the subject under discussion.

    b. Is able and willing to reason well.

    c. Is not lying.

Why should we make these assumptions? If someone with whom we are deliberating does not satisfy them, then there's no point in reasoning with him or her. The Principle of Rational Discussion summarizes those conditions without which reasoning together is pointless.

Consider (a). I leave my car at the auto repair shop because it's running badly. Later in the afternoon I return. The mechanic tells me I need a new fuel injector. I ask, "Are you sure I need one?" That sounds like an invitation for her to convince me. But she shouldn't try to use an argument. I don't have any idea how my engine works, and she might as well be speaking Greek. She should try to educate me or ask me to take her word on trust rather than reasoning.

Consider (b). Sometimes a person intends not to reason well. Like the demagogic politician or talk-show host, these people want to convince us without good reason and will not accept our arguments, no matter how good they are. There is no point in reasoning with such a person except to reveal those appeals to unreason.

Or we may encounter a person who is temporarily unable or unwilling to reason well, say, a person who is upset, or in love, or drunk. Again, it makes no sense at such a time to try to reason with such a person: calm him or her, address his or her emotions, and leave reasoning for another time.

Then again we might find ourselves with someone who wants to reason well but can't seem to follow an argument. Why try to reason with him? Offer him a copy of my *Critical Thinking*.

What about (c)? If we find that the other person is lying, not just a little white lie but continuously lying, there's no point in reasoning with him or her unless to uncover those lies.

It is not charitable to assume the Principle of Rational Discussion for someone with whom we are reasoning. When we sit down to play chess with someone, we don't say we are giving her the benefit of the doubt that she knows how to play chess. If we discover that she does not know or will not abide by the rules of the game, we stop playing. The Principle of Rational Discussion summarizes the rules for reasoning together.

Example 57   Dick: Cats are really dangerous pets. Look at all the evidence. See, it says so here in this medical journal, and it lists all the diseases you can catch from them, even schizophrenia they think. You know that lots of your friends get sick from cat allergies. And remember how Puff scratched Zoe last week? You can't deny it.

Suzy: OK, OK, I believe what you've said. So you can reason well like Dr. E. Still I don't believe that cats are dangerous pets.

Analysis Suzy recognizes that Dick has given a good argument for cats being dangerous pets, but she still doesn't believe it. She's not judiciously suspending judgment; she's just unwilling to reason about her beloved cats.

The Mark of Irrationality If you recognize that an argument is good, then it is irrational not to accept the conclusion.

But what if you hear arguments for both sides, and you can't find a flaw in either? Then you should suspend judgment on whether the claim is true until you can investigate more. That's the principle of Suspending Judgment we saw before.

By adopting the Principle of Rational Discussion we can formulate a guide for repairing and evaluating arguments.

The Guide to Repairing Arguments

The Guide to Repairing Arguments Given an (implicit) argument that is apparently defective, we are justified in *adding a premise or conclusion* if and only if all the following hold:

1. The argument becomes valid or strong.
2. The premise is plausible and is plausible to the other person.
3. The premise is more plausible than the conclusion.

If the argument is valid or strong, yet one of the premises is false or dubious, we may *delete the premise* if the argument becomes no worse.

How does the Principle of Rational Discussion justify our adopting this guide? We make the argument strong or valid first because we assume the person who made the argument can reason well, and we have fairly clear standards of when an argument is valid or strong. But we are constrained to use only premises that we and the speaker would consider plausible since we assume that he or she is not lying and knows about the subject. And though a premise that is as dubious as the conclusion may be plausible to the person making the argument, we are not allowed to add that, for it would make the argument bad, and he or she is assumed to reason well.

The Guide talks about implicit arguments. If there is a clear attempt to convince someone that a particular claim is true, and other claims are invoked in support, even if only suggested by rhetorical questions, then we may assume the other person is making an argument if it can be repaired in this manner, possibly by rewriting rhetorical questions as claims.

On the other hand, it sometimes isn't the lack of a premise, but an unnecessary premise that is a problem. We delete it and perhaps other claims that link that one to the conclusion, and accept the argument. Since the claim is not needed, we need not debate it. We assume the other person is a good reasoner, not a perfect one.

Examples of argument analysis

Example 58   Lee: I was wondering what kind of pet Dick has.
              It must be a dog.
         Maria: How do you know?
         Lee: Because I heard it barking last night.

Analysis   Maria shouldn't dismiss Lee's reasoning just because the link from premises to conclusion is missing. She should ask what claim(s) are needed to make it strong, since by the Principle of Rational Discussion she assumes Lee intends to and is able to reason well. The obvious premise to add is "All pets that bark are dogs." But Maria knows that's false (seals, foxes, parrots) and can assume that Lee does, too, since he's supposed to know about the subject. So she tries "Almost all pets that bark are dogs." That's plausible, and with it the argument is strong and good.

We first try to make the argument valid or strong because we don't need to know what the speaker was thinking in order to do so. Then we can ask whether that claim is plausible and whether it would be plausible to the other person. By first trying to make the argument valid or strong, we can show the other person what he or she needs to assume to make the argument good.

Example 59   No dog meows. So Spot does not meow.

Analysis   "Spot is a dog" is the only premise that will make this
a valid or strong argument. So we add that. Since that's true, the
argument is good.

We don't add "Spot barks." That's true, too, and likely obvious to
the person who stated the argument, but it doesn't make the argument
any better. So adding it violates requirement (1) of the Guide. We
repair only as needed.

Example 60   All professors teach. So Ms. Han is a professor.

Analysis   The obvious claim to add is "Ms. Han teaches." But
then the argument is still weak: Ms. Han could be an instructor, or a
part-time lecturer, or a graduate student. The argument can't be
repaired because the obvious premise to add makes it weak.

Example 61   Dr. E has a dog Anubis. So Anubis barks.

Analysis   We can't make this valid by adding "All dogs bark"
because we know that's false. We could make it stronger by adding
"Anubis is not a basenji" and "Anubis didn't have her vocal cords cut."
Those would rule out a lot of possibilities where Anubis is a dog but
doesn't bark. And why not add "Anubis scares away the electric meter
reader every month"? Or we could add . . . . That's creative writing,
not argument analysis. We can't just make up just anything to add to
the argument to make it stronger or valid. We have no reason to
believe those claims are true.

The only premise we can add here is a blanket one that's plausible
and rules out lots of possibilities without specifying any one of them:
"Almost all dogs bark." Then the argument is good.

Example 62   Dr. E is a good teacher because he gives fair exams.

Analysis   The unstated premise needed to make this valid or
strong is "Almost any teacher who gives fair exams is a good teacher."
That gives a strong argument. But it's not plausible: a teacher could
copy fair exams from the instructor's manual. The argument can't be
repaired because the obvious premise to add to make the argument
strong or valid is false or dubious.

But can't you make it strong by adding, say, "Dr. E gives great
explanations," "Dr. E is amusing," "Dr. E never misses class," . . . ?
Yes, all those are true, and perhaps obvious to the person. But adding

those doesn't repair this argument — it makes a whole new argument. We don't put words in someone's mouth.

Example 63 Wanda to Suzy: Sure you'll get a passing grade in English. After all, you paid tuition to take the course.

Analysis The argument is weak — and it is an argument: the last sentence is meant as reason to believe the first. But there's no obvious repair: it's false that anyone who pays tuition for a course will pass it. Wanda apparently can't reason. We don't bother to repair this one.

Example 64 Dick: It's a really bad idea to cut down all those old-growth trees there.
Tom: What are you talking about? Are you going to let those tree-huggers tell us what to do? It's about time we took charge of our own land here instead of the federal government pushing us around.

Analysis Tom is making an argument (the second question is rhetorical):

Environmentalists should not be allowed to tell us what to do.
The federal government should not be allowed to tell us what to do.
Therefore, we should go ahead and allow logging in old-growth forests.

When the argument is put this way, it seems obvious to us that Tom has confused whether we have the right to cut down the forest with whether we should allow the forest to be cut down.

Sometimes people say an argument like Tom's is bad because his premises are irrelevant to the conclusion. They say an argument is bad if in response to one or more premises your reaction is "What's that got to do with anything?" or "So?"

What would you do if someone told you a claim in an argument you made is irrelevant? You'd try to show it is relevant by adding more premises to link it to the conclusion. The trouble is that the premises needed to make the claim relevant are not obvious to the other person. When we say that a premise is irrelevant to the conclusion, all we're saying is that it doesn't make the argument any better, and we can't see how to add anything plausible that would link it to the conclusion. And when we say that all the premises are irrelevant,

we're saying that we can't even imagine how to repair the argument.
A premise is ***irrelevant*** if you can delete it and the argument isn't any
worse.[21]

Example 65   You're going to vote for the Green Party candidate for
President? Don't you realize that means your vote will be wasted?

    Analysis   Where's the argument here? These are just two
questions.

    If you heard this, you'd certainly think that the speaker is trying to
convince you to believe "You shouldn't vote for the Green Party
candidate for President." And the speaker is giving a reason to believe
that: "Your vote will be wasted." This is an implicit argument.

    The argument sounds pretty good, though something is missing.
A visitor from Denmark may not know "The Green Party candidate
doesn't have a chance of winning." But even then she could ask "So?"
The argument is missing the a link from the premises to the conclusion.
We'd have to fill in the argument further: "If you vote for someone
who doesn't have a chance of winning, then your vote will be wasted."
And when we add that premise, we see the argument that used such
"obvious" premises is really not very good. Why should we believe
that if you vote for someone who doesn't stand a chance of winning
then your vote is wasted? If that were true, then who wins is the only
important result of an election, rather than, say, making a position
understood by the electorate. At best we can say that when the unstated
premises are added, we get an argument one of whose premises needs
a substantial argument to convince us that it's true. Trying to repair
an argument can lead us to unstated assumptions about which the real
debate should be.

Example 66   Cats are more likely than dogs to carry diseases harmful
to humans. Cats kill songbirds and can kill people's pets. Cats disturb
people at night with their screeching and clattering in garbage cans.
Cats leave paw prints on cars and will sleep in unattended cars. Cats
are not as pleasant as dogs and are owned only by people who have
Satanic affinities. So there should be a leash law for cats just as much
as for dogs.

    Analysis   This letter to the editor is going pretty well until the
next to last sentence. That claim is a bit dubious, and the argument will
be better without it. So we should delete it. Then, by adding some

obvious claims that link the premises to the conclusion by ruling out other possibilities, we'll have a good argument.

Example 67 In a famous speech, Martin Luther King Jr. said:

> "I have a dream that one day this nation will rise up and live out the true meaning of its creed: 'We hold these truths to be self-evident— that all men are created equal.' . . . I have a dream that one day even the state of Mississippi, a desert state sweltering with the heat of injustice and oppression, will be transformed into an oasis of freedom and justice. I have a dream that my four little children will one day live in a nation where they will not be judged by the color of their skin but by the content of their character."
>
> . . . King is also presenting a logical argument . . . the argument might be stated as follows: "America was founded on the principle that all men are created equal. This implies that people should not be judged by skin color, which is an accident of birth, but rather by what they make of themselves ('the content of their character'). To be consistent with this principle, America should treat black people and white people alike."   David Kelley, *The Art of Reasoning*, p. 114

Analysis The rewriting of this passage is too much of a stretch— putting words in someone's mouth—to be justified. Where did David Kelley get "This implies . . ."? Stating my dreams and hoping others will share them is not an argument. Martin Luther King, Jr. knew how to argue well and could do so when he wanted. We're not going to make his words more respectable by pretending they're an argument. Not every good attempt to convince is an argument.

Example 68 Alcoholism is a disease, not a character flaw. People are genetically predisposed to be addicted to alcohol. An alcoholic should not be fired or imprisoned, but should be given treatment.

Treatment centers should be established because it is too difficult to overcome the addiction to alcohol all by oneself. The encourage- ment and direction of others is what is needed to help people, for alcoholics can find the power within themselves to fight and triumph over their addiction.

Analysis On the face of it, "Alcoholism is a disease, not a character flaw" contradicts "Alcoholics can find the power within themselves to fight and triumph over their addiction." Both these claims are premises needed for the conclusion "Treatment centers should be established." When premises contradict each other and can't be deleted, there's no way to repair the argument.

Example 69   U.S. citizens are independent souls, and they tend to dislike
being forced to do anything. The compulsory nature of Social
Security therefore has been controversial since the program's
beginnings. Many conservatives argue that Social Security should be
made voluntary, rather than compulsory.

J. Brux and J. Cowen, *Economic Issues and Policy*, p. 271

Analysis   The first two sentences look like an argument. But the
first sentence is too vague to be a claim. And even if it could be made
precise, we'd have an explanation, not an attempt to convince. We
don't try to repair what is not an argument.

Example 70   It is only for the sake of profit that any man employs a capital
in the support of industry; and he will always, therefore, endeavour to employ it
in the support of that industry of which the produce is likely to be of greatest
value, or to exchange for the greatest quantity either of money or of other
goods.   Adam Smith, *The Wealth of Nations*, IV.II.8

Analysis   The argument is valid. But its single premise is false.
Lots of other considerations about where to invest money matter to
many people: convenience, social responsibility, ... So there's no
way to repair it, and it's bad.

We've seen how to repair some arguments. Just as important,
we've seen that some arguments can't be repaired. For practical
applications as well as to avoid the mistakes we saw in the discussion
of a principle of charity, we need clear conditions for when we should
not attempt to reshape what is said into a good argument.

Unrepairable Arguments   We cannot repair a (purported) argument if
any of the following hold:

- There is no argument there.
- The argument is so lacking in coherence there's nothing
  obvious to add.
- A premise is false or dubious, or several premises together
  are contradictory and cannot be deleted without making the
  argument weak.
- The obvious premise to add would make the argument weak.
- Any obvious premise to add to make the argument valid or
  strong is false.
- The conclusion is clearly false.

Does every good argument require a general principle as premise?

When we try to repair an argument, should we be looking for a general principle in order to make the argument valid or strong? Some people believe that for an argument to be good a universal law or some universal claim is needed as a premise.[22] That view, however, is wrong.

Example 71 Tom: Maria is a widow.
   Lee: So Maria was married.

Analysis As analyzed in Example 35, Lee's argument satisfies the conditions for an argument to be good. To insist that the argument is lacking the obvious premise "Anyone who is a widow was married" is to misconstrue the role of definitions in reasoning, for that amounts to taking a part of the definition of "divorced" as a premise. Definitions are what we use as background for our reasoning, for we assume that the person with whom we are reasoning speaks our language. The only reason to insist on such a premise is to enforce the requirement that every good argument must have a universal claim as premise.

Example 72 George is a duck or George is a goose. George is not a duck. So George is a goose.

Analysis This is a good argument. We can see from its form that it's valid. This amounts to saying that by understanding the words "or" and "not" we can see that it is impossible for the premises to be true and conclusion false, and by the Principle of Rational Discussion we can assume that anyone with whom we are reasoning can, too. There is no general principle needed to make this argument valid. Were we to add one about the nature of arguments of this form, we would be embarking on an infinite regress.[23]

If every good argument needs a universal premise, what about generalizations from many particulars? They are at best strong arguments. Some say that every generalization requires a general principle in order to be good, an assumption about the uniformity of nature. But, as discussed in "Generalizing" in this volume, for any specific generalization, no candidate for such a general principle is more plausible than the conclusion. Moreover, to take such a principle amounts to incorporating an assumption about how to reason well into the premises of our arguments, which again threatens an infinite regress. Of course one could say that these problems simply show that a generalization can't be a good argument.

Sometimes, though, a general principle is needed as a premise.

Example 72   Dick: Cats urinate in the house. Cats kill songbirds. Cats barf up hairballs in the house. So all in all, cats are unpleasant and unsuitable as pets.

Harry: All your premises are true, but what have they got to do with the conclusion? Am I supposed to have some insight into how the conclusion follows from it? How are these premises relevant?

Dick: Oh, come on. Even if you think that one of the premises isn't enough, each one adds more reason to believe the conclusion.

Harry: Even if each gives more reason to believe the conclusion, which I doubt, all together they still don't make a strong argument.

Analysis   If Dick were to take Harry's objection seriously he'd have to show why he thinks the argument is strong. The first premise is relevant because he believes "Any animal that urinates in the house is unsuitable as a pet." The second requires a premise like, "Animals that kill songbirds are usually bad pets." Or those repairs might be too much and only all the premises together should be covered by some claim such as "Almost any animal that urinates in the house, kills songbirds, and barfs up hairballs in the house is unsuitable as a pet."

The latter is plausible if and only if the argument is strong. By replying to Harry, Dick will have to make his unstated assumptions explicit. This is not to say that every argument requires a general claim to be good, but that ruling out possibilities will often lead to a statement of a general claim that makes explicit unstated assumptions. Piling up lots of reasons for a conclusion without linking them to the conclusion is nothing better than a series of weak arguments.

Making explicit the assumptions that show our arguments to be valid or strong is part of the methodology we adopt in repairing and evaluating arguments which we codified in the principle that an argument is not strong by default. Without that we are left with only inarticulate pointing and insight as to why an argument is valid or strong.

Carl Wellman disagrees. He says that there are "conductive" arguments that require a different standard of evaluation in which no general principle is needed:

> That sort of reasoning in which (1) a conclusion about some individual case (2) is drawn nonconclusively (3) from one or more premises about the same case (4) without any appeal to other cases.[24]

Trudy Govier discusses the history of this idea and endorses it. The closest she gets to a definition is the following:

> In a conductive argument no one premise deductively entails the conclusion, nor do the premises entail the conclusion when considered together. The premises count for the conclusion by being relevant to it, in a sense of "relevant" less than sufficiency. The method by which we assess a conductive argument is not to test for deductive validity, but rather to ask ourselves whether the premises are relevant, how much support they give to the conclusion, and whether unmentioned factors that are also relevant to the conclusion "outweigh" the premises. We may also consider further cases to test claims of relevance. The conclusion is not a generalization from cases, as it would be in an enumerative induction. Nor does it presume empirical regularities among considered cases or the kind of background empirical knowledge needed for explanatory or causal inductive reasoning. Whether X is relevant to Y, in these contexts, is a conceptual, normative, or 'criterial' issue.[25]

This requires a much clearer explanation of relevance, which she does not provide. Example 72, perhaps with more premises about the behavior of cats, seems a perfect example of such an argument, yet we saw that piling up lots of reasons for a conclusion without linking any one of them to the conclusion is just a series of weak arguments. In response to each independent premise one could ask, "So?" Lots of weak arguments do not sum up to a strong argument.[26]

Some guide for analyzing arguments is essential. Saying that a conductive argument can be good, and we can see that is so through weighing up the pros and cons, is just to say that we need not try to make explicit our unstated assumptions when challenged. That contradicts a fundamental principle of reasoning well: *Uncover the unstated assumptions so we can discuss those*.

Further, even if some kind of general principle is needed, it needn't be a universal claim, unless we reject strong arguments: "Almost all dogs bark" is a general principle. Only an examination of the use of general principles in different kinds of inferences might help us to be more explicit about their nature. About all we can say here is that an argument requires a general principle if all the following apply:

> It is not a generalization.
>
> We have not already agreed that any argument of that form is valid or strong.
>
> It is not valid due solely to the meaning of the words in it.
>
> It is not obviously valid or strong as stated.

The general principle is a claim that clearly makes the argument valid or strong. But this just amount to saying that every argument should be repaired according to the Guide to Repairing Arguments.

It also seems that whether one requires a general principle as premise in order for an argument to be good depends on one's metaphysics. An empiricist takes only claims about personal experience to be plausible without argument, except for the few general principles that govern his or her metaphysics or criteria of good reasoning, such as "Any claim that is not about personal experience requires justification."[27] Hence, any other general claim an empiricist accepts must be arrived at from reasoning that relies, in the first instance, on claims that are not general. An empiricist, it seems, will have to accept arguments that generalize from particulars to general claims as being acceptable, or else accept no general principles beyond those that establish his or her metaphysics and criteria of reasoning.

In contrast, a subjective idealist might take some general claims as plausible without reasoning. These would include not only general claims about metaphysics, such as "All personal experience is an illusion," but also claims that are used in more ordinary reasoning, such as "All electrons have spin." Only reasoning from general claims, an idealist might say, can one arrive at claims about particular things. So, it seems, an idealist will have to reject arguments that generalize from particulars to general claims as being acceptable reasoning. General principles that many of us might employ such as "Almost all dogs bark" could be considered by an idealist to be too tainted by experience to be useful in reasoning well. In that case, only universal claims and only valid arguments would be acceptable to such an idealist.

Conclusion

We first considered what things are true or false: claims. Then we looked at the idea of one claim following from one or more other claims: inferences. Then we focused on inferences that are intended to show that the conclusion is true: arguments.

A good argument is one that gives good reason to believe that its conclusion is true. So a good argument must have plausible premises that are more plausible than the conclusion. And the conclusion must follow from the premises.

Two standards are proposed for when the conclusion of an argument follows from the premises. If an argument is valid then the conclusion definitely follows. If an argument is strong, it would seem that the conclusion follows, too, but some dispute that. Considering examples and the reasons for doubt, we saw that if strong arguments are not good by some impersonal standard, then they are nonetheless good enough for reasoning in our ordinary lives.

Many arguments we encounter are not good as stated but can be repaired to be good. Clear standards can be given for how to repair an argument and when we can classify an argument as unrepairable, based on assumptions we make about those with whom we reason.

Good reason to believe, not "knowledge," is the issue. Perhaps we have knowledge but are not ever certain that we do. But we can determine whether we have good reason to believe. Perhaps only God, or the gods, or Dog who smells all have knowledge, can see the true nature of things. We should strive to know as He, She, or They do. But that is a goal, and we might never even know we have attained it.

We can treat all our "knowledge" as provisional. That is only to accept that we could be wrong, admitting our fallibility, our human limitations. But it would not seem to have any significance in our daily lives other than making us more willing to revise our opinions. Looking for good reason to believe rather than knowledge is acceptance of humility and our human limitations.

Appendix   The asymmetry of showing validity vs. showing invalidity

It is sometimes said that there is a significant difference in how difficult it is to show that an argument is invalid compared to showing that it is valid.[28] To show an argument is valid, the story goes, all we have to do is exhibit a valid form of argument that it instantiates. For example,

> All dogs bark.
> Juney is a dog.
> So Juney barks.

is an instance of the valid form:

> All A are B.
> *a* is A.
> So *a* is B.

Hence, the argument is valid. But it is much harder to show an argument is invalid, since then we would have to show that it instantiates no valid form. And that would mean surveying infinitely many possibilities.

This view places too much reliance on formal logic. Are we to say that "Juney is barking loudly, so Juney is barking" is difficult to show valid because it does not instantiate a valid form in a formal logic? And are we to say that it is difficult to show that the following is invalid because we would have to survey all valid forms to make sure it does not instantiate any one of them?

> All dogs bark.
> Juney barks.
> So Juney is a dog.

It is easy to show this argument is invalid: Exhibit a particular way the premises could be true and conclusion false. For example, Juney could be a seal while the first premise could be true if all non-barking dogs were to die tomorrow. There is an asymmetry, but what is difficult one way is easy another.

	Valid	*Invalid*
Formal	Easy if there is a valid form.	Hard if have to survey all forms.
Informal	Hard if have to survey all possibilities.	Easy if there is a counterexample.

For strong arguments, the asymmetry seems worse. It is easy to show an argument is weak. All we have to do is give a likely description of how the world could be in which the premises could be true and conclusion false. But it is hard to show that an argument is strong. We have to survey all possibilities in which the premises are true and show that all the ones we can imagine in which the conclusion is false are very unlikely. Not only do we have to survey all possibilities, we have to be very good at deciding what is or is not likely.

But sometimes it is easy to show that an argument is strong. In some of the examples above, all we have to do is check whether the following meta-claim is true: "Nothing else is known by us about a that would distinguish it from everything else in A as regards whether a is B."

NOTES

1. (p. 3) These last two examples show that in the definition of "claim," "declarative sentence" rather than "part of speech" is not apt, though I used that in my previous work. Worse, a declarative sentence is usually defined to be a sentence that makes a claim or that is true or false.

2. (p. 6) Brian Skyrms in *Choice & Chance: An Introduction to Inductive Logic* tries to avoid intentions in his definition of "argument" :

> An argument is a list of *statements*, one of which is designated the conclusion and the rest of which are designated as premises. p. 1–2

Skyrms defines "statement" as a sentence "that makes a definite factual claim." It would seem, then, that sentences are not claims but "make" them, but in what way he does not say. Nor does he explain what the difference is between a factual claim and a claim that is not factual; he doesn't even say what a claim is. In any case, his definition of "argument" still relies on intentions, since only a person can designate a claim as a conclusion. The bigger problem with this definition is that it allows for a report in a newspaper to be an argument, since there is nothing to prevent someone from understanding "conclusion" as "topic sentence of the report." When Skyrms begins to use the notion of argument in his book, he does invoke the intention of the speaker.

3. (p. 6) Both of which are false.

4. (p. 7) Some have said that an argument is good if it would convince a rational person. But the notion of good argument is part of what constitutes rationality, as I explain in "Rationality" in this volume.

5. (p. 10) See "Truth and Reasoning" in *Prescriptive Reasoning*.

6. (p. 12) The usual definition of "begging the question" is that a premise or premises restates or reiterates the conclusion or there is circularity. Those ideas are hard to make clear and are covered by this definition, which picks out a class of arguments we need to discuss anyway and which has long been considered important. Sextus Empiricus in *Outlines of Pyrrhonism* (2:140) reports on a Stoic view (as translated by Benson Mates in *The Skeptic Way*):

> Again, of the true arguments some are probative and some are not probative; the probative are those validly concluding something non-evident from things that are pre-evident, and the non-probative are those that are not of this sort. For example, such an argument as this:
>> If it is day, it is light.
>> It is day.
>> Therefore, it is light.

> is not probative, for its conclusion, that it is light, is pre-evident.

See also the discussion of this point and this example in Chapter 7 of

Definition and Induction by Kisor Kumar Chakrabarti. Brendan Gillon in "Logic in Classical Indian Philosophy" reports that the same class was studied in the classical tradition in India:

> In all likelihood, included here [in the *Caraka-samhita*] are both cases where the premises of the argument can be true but the conclusion false—formal fallacies—as well as cases where an argument, though formally valid, is nonetheless unpersuasive, since, for example, its ground (*hetu*) is as controversial as its conclusion. p. 8

Steven M. Cahn in *Fate, Logic, and Time* suggests an apparently stronger criterion: the premises of a good argument have to be more plausible than both the conclusion and the denial of the conclusion:

> All these arguments against man's free will have seemed convincing to many thinkers. However, they are all open to one vital objection: the premise of each argument can be reasonably denied. It can be reasonably denied that every event has a cause, or that a man must always choose what he believes to be best, or that a man's subconscious always controls his conscious decisions. Though each of these may seem plausible at first, it could be reasonably maintained that it is more plausible that man has free will than that any of these premises is true. . . .
>
> In order to prove any proposition *P*, one must adopt premises from which *P* can be deduced, such that more evidence exists in support of the premises than in support of the denial of *P*. If more evidence exists in support of the denial of *P* than in support of the premises, one can simply deny *P* and deny the premises. . . .
>
> Any proposition can be "proven" if one adopts suitable premises. The difficulty in any proof is to find premises which yield the desired conclusion and which are more plausible than the denial of that conclusion. pp. 7–8

In the examples Cahn gives the problem isn't that the premise isn't more plausible than the denial of the conclusion, it's that the premise is not plausible at all. I don't know an example of an argument that is valid or strong and whose premises are plausible and more plausible than the conclusion, yet one of the premises is less plausible than the denial of the conclusion.

7. (p. 15) In giving hundreds of examples of arguments in *Critical Thinking* I could provide only a very few valid ones we might use in our daily lives, much less valid ones with obviously true premises.

8. (p. 17) *A System of Logic*, III.III.3 (p. 227).

9. (p. 22) Rudolf Carnap in *Logical Foundations of Probability*, p. 211, talks about knowledge as the basis of evaluation:

Suppose that inductive logic supplies a simple result of the form
'$c(h,e) = r$', where h and e are two given sentences and r
is a given real number. How is this result to be applied to a given
knowledge situation? This question is answered by the following
rule, which is not a rule of inductive logic but of the methodology of
induction:

> If e expresses the total knowledge of X at the time t, that is
> to say, his total knowledge of the results of his observations,
> then X is justified at this time to believe h to the degree r,
> and hence to bet on h with a betting quotient not higher than r.

One of the decisive points in this rule is the fact that it lays down the
following stipulation:

> *Requirement of total evidence*: in the application of inductive logic
> to a given knowledge situation, the total evidence available must be
> taken as basis for determining the degree of confirmation.

This last requirement seems more apt if by "evidence" we understand those
claims which we are taking into account that we have good reason to believe.
Then the attempt to make explicit the assumptions on which we base the
determination of the strength of an argument can replace Carnap's requirement
of "total evidence available."

A platonist could say that it's objective whether an argument is strong, we
just don't know how to use that objective standard and are stuck in a subjective
methodology of determining the strength of arguments. But such an objective
scale will not help us reason well.

10. (p. 27) Examples of doubt about the validity of specific inferences
arise regularly in mathematics, as discussed in "Mathematics as the Art
of Abstraction" in *Reasoning in the Sciences* in this series.

11. (p. 28) This is confused skepticism because it is not applied thoroughly
to all our reasoning but only selectively to one particular aspect of it. Compare
Ludwig Wittgenstein, *On Certainty*, paragraph 338:

> But imagine people who were never quite certain of these things, but
> said that they were *very* probably so, and that it did not pay to doubt
> them. Such a person, then, would say in my situation: "It is extremely
> unlikely that I have ever been on the moon," etc., etc. *How* would the
> life of these people differ from ours? For there *are* people who say
> that it is merely extremely probable that water over a fire will boil
> and not freeze, and that therefore strictly speaking what we consider
> impossible is only improbable. What difference does that make in
> their lives? Isn't it just that they talk rather more about certain things
> than the rest of us?

12. (p. 12) I am not suggesting that we need to have strong arguments to act. We need not reason, and even if we do reason, our acting on the basis of that reasoning need not show that we do or should believe, as I discuss in "Rationality" in this volume. I am only saying that *if* we want reasoning to play a substantial role in our lives, it seems we will need to accept that some strong arguments are good.

13. (p. 30) A principle of charity was originally proposed as an aid to or explanation of how to translate from an unknown tongue. It came to be applied, in one form or another, to the general problem of ascribing beliefs. Christopher Gauker, "The Principle of Charity," provides a short summary of various versions and surveys the discussions of what warrant we have for adopting them.

14. (p. 30) *Practical Reasoning*, pp. 18–19.

15. (p. 30) *Reason and Argument*, p. 115.

16. (p. 30) *Critical Reasoning*, p. 22.

17. (p. 30) *Attacking Faulty Reasoning*, p. 6.

18. (p. 31) Trudy Govier in "A New Approach to Charity" discusses this type of principle of charity and shows that neither an ethical, prudential, nor epistemic warrant can serve to justify it. She also presents the history of these principles in relation to the principle of charity in semantics
   Jonathan Berg, in "Interpreting Arguments," discusses various versions of the principle of charity with somewhat stronger warrants. He proposes criteria similar to what I propose below. For instance, he says, "Assume that the speaker is not grossly deficient in either general knowledge or logical competence, i.e., that he would not make wildly absurd claims or inferences."
   There is also a discussion of the principle of charity in "Relativism in its place" by Steven Lukes. In the context of analyzing translations he comes to a view (pp. 263–265) similar to my Principle of Rational Discussion below.

19. (p. 32) "Fallacies and the Evaluation of Reasoning."

20. (p. 32) See "Explanations" in *Cause and Effect, Conditionals, Explanations* in this series of books.

21. (p. 38) Aristotle had a similar view of relevance in his "fallacy of false cause" (*De Sophisticis Elenchis*, 167b, 21–27 and *Analytica Priora*, 65a36–65b12). The Federal Rules of Evidence (U.S., 1999) state as rule 401:

> "Relevant evidence" means evidence having any tendency to make the existence of any fact that is of consequence to the determination of the action more probable or less probable than it would be without the evidence.

John Maynard Keynes gives a similar definition in *A Treatise on Probability*:

The simplest definition of Irrelevance is as follows: h_1 is irrelevant to x on evidence h, if the probability of x on evidence hh_1 is the same as its probability on evidence h. But . . . theoretically preferable [is]: h_1 is irrelevant to x on evidence h, if there is no proposition, inferrible from $h_1 h$ but not from h, such that its addition to evidence h affects the probability of x. p. 55

22. (p. 41) That assumption usually goes with the assumption that a good argument should be valid. See Trudy Govier, "Is a Theory of Argument Possible?", section 3, pp. 22–27, for a discussion of this view.

23. (p. 41) Compare Lewis Carroll, "What the Tortoise Said to Achilles."

24. (p. 43) *Challenge and Response: Justification in Ethics.*

25. (p. 43) "Two Unreceived Views about Reasoning and Argument," p. 70.

26. (p. 43) In that paper, Govier offers another example:

"Blacks are equal to whites because they are as healthy as whites, they are biologically very similar to whites, they are as intelligent as whites, and they share basic needs with whites." Whatever the substantive merits of this argument, it is based on separately non-conclusively relevant premises cited to support a conclusion and it is the sort of argument where 'cons' should be acknowledged and 'weighed' with the 'pros'. p. 69

The quotes around the word "weighed" conceal a lack of a general approach to analyzing arguments. On the face of it this argument requires an unstated premise like "When one group of people is as healthy as another, as intelligent as another, and share the same basic needs, then the two groups are equal." But that won't do. At best that sentence might be taken as a definition of "equal," except that it uses notions for which there is no known standard: intelligence and basic needs. This example is not a good or bad conductive argument. It is not even a hopelessly weak argument. It is so vague that it is no argument at all.

27. (p. 44) I do not see how an empiricist could take that claim as a generalization from particulars, though I suspect that empiricists will try. When they do we'll have to look at what general principles they are assuming that govern what they count as good reasoning.

28. (p. 46) See, e.g., Maurice Finocchiaro, "The Positive Versus the Negative Evaluation of Arguments."

Fallacies

The notion of a fallacy can be a useful tool in analyzing arguments.
But the usual definitions are at best unclear and not helpful. Setting
out a general approach to argument analysis will lead us to a definition
of "fallacy" that gives guidance for when to classify a mistake in
reasoning as a fallacy and how to use that notion in argument analysis.

The classical view of fallacies

What is a fallacy? Here is what C. L. Hamblin says:

> A fallacious argument, as almost every account from Aristotle
> onward tells you, is one that *seems to be valid* but *is not* so.[1]

But to whom is the argument supposed to seem valid? When a
student spots that an argument is bad, should we tell her that the
argument is no longer a fallacy, since it doesn't seem good to her?

We classify arguments that are clearly bad, in our estimation, as
fallacies. So neither to us nor to even lightly trained reasoners do these
arguments appear good. We cannot appeal to the judgment of the man
in the street accepting an argument as good when it is not, for then we
should have to employ polling agencies to tell us which arguments are
fallacies. And saying that an argument has the potential to mislead is
no criterion at all. The definition handed down to us over centuries is
condescending, is not in accord with our practice, and yields no
effective criterion for what is or is not a fallacy.

In practice, lists of types of bad arguments are produced, some interesting analyses of particular types of bad arguments are made, but the definition is never actually employed. What definitions are used and what applications are made of the notion of fallacy are at best confusing.

The confusions and errors are symptomatic of deficiencies in the methods of argument analysis that are offered. To revise the notion of fallacy to be a useful tool requires a clear and useful notion of argument analysis. That is what I have presented in the essay "Arguments" in this volume, which is the background I'll assume here.

Current views of fallacies

The classical view again

There is an additional problem with the classical view of fallacies. Compare the following two arguments:

> All dogs bark.
> Juney barks.
> Therefore, Juney is a dog.

> Almost all dogs bark.
> Juney barks.
> Therefore, Juney is a dog.

If the first argument is a fallacy, which I suggest below, then so is the second for the same structural reasons, substituting "strong" for "valid." But the standard definition doesn't allow the term "fallacy" to be applied to arguments that are intended to be strong and not valid.[2]

The pragma-dialectical view

Frans van Eemeren and Rob Grootendorst define fallacies as mistakes in speech communication.

> A fallacy is a hindrance or impediment to the resolution of a disagreement, and the specific nature of each of the fallacies depends on the exact manner in which it interferes with the resolution process.

> Making an argument pragmatically presupposes a standpoint and at least the potential for opposition to that standpoint. In order to find out whether or not a person's opinions make sense and whether or not his reasoning holds water, he must submit them to public scrutiny.[3]

But many fallacies occur when there is no disagreement. This happens often in public, and almost always when one reasons with oneself. Appealing to potential disagreements is no guide to when one might encounter a fallacy, since there is always, in all talk, the possibility of a disagreement.

Further, it is not whether reasoning "holds water" nor whether opinions "make sense." Fallacies are concerned with belief and truth in the context of an argument. Van Eemeren and Grootendorst continue:

> The argumentation is appropriate only if it is capable of accommo-
> dating the critical reactions of a rational judge. In order to determine
> whether this is the case, the argumentation is to be viewed as part of a
> critical discussion conducted in accordance with a problem-valid and
> conventionally valid discussion procedure. The problem-validity of a
> discussion procedure depends on its efficiency in achieving a resolu-
> tion to the disagreement and its efficacy in furthering the resolution
> process while avoiding "false" resolutions. The conventional validity
> depends on the intersubjective acceptability of the procedure. The
> procedure provides a set of standards for rational judgment.[4]

I do not know what "critical reactions of a rational judge" are, nor "rational judgment," nor "standpoints" if those are not explained in terms of truth and the notions of strong and valid arguments. Van Eemeren and Grootendorst recognize that notions of reasoning must be incorporated somewhere in their analysis. They offer rules, one of which is:

> A party may not regard a standpoint as conclusively defended if the
> defense does not take place by means of an appropriate argumenta-
> tion scheme that is correctly applied.[5]

But if an "appropriate argumentation scheme" is meant as some valid or strong scheme of argument, then the rule is too strong. It would classify as bad all reasoning of mathematicians who leave steps to the reader.

The role of communication should not replace the use and dis-
tinctions of argument analysis in analyzing fallacies. The nature of dialectic can be incorporated with just the definition of "argument" and the Principle of Rational Discussion.

Fallacies as violations of the criteria of good argument
Ralph Johnson says:

> A fallacy is an *argument* that violates one of the criteria/standards of
> good argument and that occurs with sufficient frequency in discourse
> to warrant being baptized.[6]

This is similar to what I propose below. But Johnson does not give the criteria/standards nor show how the view can be applied to decide whether an argument is a fallacy. He also presupposes a notion of relevance as part of his criteria, when relevance is one of the problems that an analysis of fallacies should explain.

T. Edward Damer offers:

A fallacy is a violation of one of the criteria of a good argument.[7]

The criteria he gives are: the premises are relevant, the premises are acceptable, the premises are sufficient grounds, and there is not an effective rebuttal. But if these criteria are to be clear, they must devolve into something like the necessary conditions for an argument to be good given in "Arguments," except for the notion of relevance, which should be explained, not assumed by a theory of fallacies. In any case, he immediately follows this definition with a variation on the classical one: "Fallacies are mistakes in reasoning that typically do not seem to be mistakes at all."

A definition of "fallacy"

I propose the following definition.

Fallacies   A *fallacy* is a bad argument of one of the types that have been agreed to be so bad as to be unrepairable.

By "agreed" I mean that the community of reasoners has explicitly pointed out the type. This need not be for the reason that Johnson gives: the type of bad argument occurs with sufficient frequency to warrant being baptized. Exhibiting the type may be a prophylactic against falling into error.

A *fallacy type* is a scheme or description of potentially infinitely many arguments. Not every argument that fits into a fallacy type need be bad, as I show in the examples below. A fallacy is an argument that fits at least one fallacy type and is actually bad.

A fallacy is a bad argument. It is not enough to say that it is a bad form of speech communication or a bad attempt to convince. The notions of truth and plausibility and of valid or strong argument are essential, as well as criteria for when an argument is unrepairable. Hence it is wrong to call the use of a loaded question or ridicule a fallacy.[8] There are many bad ways to attempt to convince people, and some criteria must be employed to distinguish them from good ways. But a theory of fallacies cannot do so for attempts to convince that are not arguments.

Fallacies can be classified into three broad categories according to the ways in which they are bad arguments.

Structural fallacies The argument has one of the forms of a bad argument type, relative to the (possibly implicit) logic we adopt.

Content fallacies The argument uses or requires via the Guide to Repairing Arguments a particular kind of premise that is typically implausible.

Violations of the rules of rational discussion

I will discuss each of these in turn.[9]

Structural fallacies
Some arguments are bad because of their form. But the Guide to Repairing Arguments does not tell us to take as unrepairable just any invalid argument. Many arguments that are invalid are nonetheless strong, and some arguments that have the form of a weak argument may nonetheless be repairable.

We classify as unrepairable due solely to their form those invalid arguments that make us believe the person is not capable of reasoning well (for the moment, perhaps) because they mimic a valid or strong form but are usually weak. Here are the ones I discuss in *Critical Thinking*.

fallacy type	*similar type of valid or strong argument*
affirming the consequent	*modus ponens*
If A, then B.	If A, then B.
B	A
Therefore, A.	Therefore, B.
denying the antecedent	*modus tollens*
If A, then B.	If A, then B.
not A	not B
Therefore, not B.	Therefore, not A.

fallacy type	*similar type of valid or strong argument*
arguing backwards with "all"	
All A are B.	All A are B.
a is B.	a is A.
Therefore, x is A.	Therefore, a is B.
reasoning in a chain with "some"	*reasoning in a chain with "all"*
Some A are B.	All A are B.
Some B are C.	All B are C.
Therefore, some A are C.	Therefore, all A are C.
arguing backwards with "no"	
All A are B.	All A are B.
No C is A.	No C is B.
Therefore, no C is B.	Therefore, no C is A.
arguing backwards with "almost all"	*direct way of reasoning with "almost all"*
Almost all S are P.	Almost all S are P.
a is P.	a is S.
Therefore, a is S.	Therefore, a is P.

reasoning in a chain with "almost all"
    Almost all S are P.
    Almost all P are Q.
    Therefore, almost all S are Q.

It is not that these forms of argument occur with great frequency, though in my experience some of them do. What warrants us in classifying arguments of these forms as fallacies is that we are justified in taking them as unrepairable. Naming them is a useful but inessential part of that classification.

When someone presents an argument that fits one of these fallacy types, we assume that he or she is confused about how to reason. We don't try to repair it.

Content fallacies

Many arguments are bad because they use or require for repair a very dubious premise. Usually we have to spend some time analyzing the argument to spot what dubious premise is implicitly assumed.

But some kinds of arguments always look suspicious. When we spot one of those, we look for the generic premise the argument uses or needs for repair. If it is false, the argument is a fallacy. Here is a list of fallacy types I discuss in *Critical Thinking* along with their generic premises.[10]

Drawing the line
If you can't make the difference precise, there is no difference.

Mistaking the person (group) for the claim
(Almost) anything that _____ says about _____ is (probably) false.[11]

Mistaking the person (group) for the argument
(Almost) any argument that _____ gives about _____ is bad.

Appeal to authority
(Almost) anything that _____ says about _____ is (probably) true.

Appeal to common belief
If (almost) everyone else (in this group) believes it, then it's true.

Appeal to common practice
If (almost) everyone else (in this group) does it, then it's O.K. to do.

Phony refutation
1. _____ has done or said _____, which shows that he (she) does not believe the conclusion of his (her) own argument.
2. If someone does not believe the conclusion of his (her) own argument, then the argument is bad.

Slippery slope
If A, then B; if B, then C; . . .
This is reasoning in a chain with conditionals where one of them is false or enough of them are dubious, so the conclusion does not follow.[12]

False dilemma
> The use of any implausible "or" claim as a premise
> (sometimes an equivalent conditional is used).

Appeal to pity
> You should believe or do _____ if you feel sorry for _____ .

Appeal to fear (scare tactics)
> You should believe or do _____ if you are afraid of _____ .

Appeal to spite
> You should believe or do _____ if you are mad about what _____
> has done or believes.

Appeal to tradition
> You should believe or do _____ because it's a tradition.

Calling in your debts
> You should believe or do _____ if you owe _____ a favor.

Feel-good argument (apple polishing, wishful thinking)
> You should believe or do _____ if it makes you feel good.

Shifting the burden of proof
> I do not have to prove _____ , you have to disprove that.[13]

> This list is not meant to be exhaustive, but only illustrative.
> We now have a way to distinguish an argument that is, say,
an appeal to fear which is not a fallacy from one that is: the generic
premise is plausible.

Violations of the rules of rational discussion

Begging the question

Any argument that uses a premise that's not more plausible than the
conclusion is not a good argument. If that premise cannot be deleted
according to the Guide to Repairing Arguments, then the argument is
bad.

Strawman

If a person misrepresents your position, he is lying or wrong. If the
first, he or she no longer satisfies the conditions of the Principle of
Rational Discussion.

Arguing backwards

Arguing from the strength of an argument and the truth of its conclusion to the truth of its premises mistakes that the point of an argument is to convince that the conclusion is true.

Relevance

To classify an argument as bad because the premise or some premises are irrelevant is not to say anything useful about the argument.

Typically, a challenge that the premises of an argument are not relevant is answered by invoking further premises that link the original ones to the conclusion. And typically those further premises do indeed provide a link. Then those added premises must be evaluated. A charge that the premises of an argument are irrelevant is nothing more than an observation that the argument is not good and we cannot imagine how to repair it. It is not a category of fallacy, any more than "weak argument" is a category.

Irrelevant premises   A premise is *irrelevant* if it can be deleted and the argument is no worse.

Examples

The notion of fallacy is an extension of Unrepairable Arguments. Naming various argument types as fallacies in many cases allows us to avoid a longer argument analysis. To illustrate this, I'll present a few examples to illustrate the theory. Many more can be found in my *Critical Thinking*.

Example 1   The moon rises in the west. The moon is nearly at the horizon in the east. So the moon must be nearly ready to set.

Analysis   This is a bad argument because one of the premises is clearly false. It does not fall into any category of fallacy, nor would it be instructive to find a category for it, unless you wish to dub any argument with a clearly false premise a "clearly false premise fallacy." *Not every bad argument is a fallacy.*

Example 2   All dogs bark. Spot is a dog. So Puff meows.

Analysis   The argument is weak and there's no obvious premise we can add to make it strong or valid that does not beg the question. It is unrepairable. To say that it is an example of a fallacy of relevance is to add nothing to the analysis nor allow a quicker evaluation.

Example 3 Not every real number has a terminating decimal expansion. Therefore, there is some real number that does not have a terminating decimal expansion.

Analysis According to constructive mathematicians this is an example of a structural fallacy, although they accept the conclusion. But for classical mathematicians this is a good valid argument. Whether an argument is a fallacy depends on the methods of reasoning adopted by the community of reasoners.

Example 4 If capital punishment deterred murder, it would be justified. Since it doesn't, it isn't.

Analysis This is a clear example of denying the antecedent. It is a fallacy. There is no reason to think the speaker is reasoning well.

Michael Burke says this is not a fallacy.[14] More generally he says:

> I will not rely on *any* principle of charity. I will need only a principle prohibiting the *opposite* of charity, one I will call (for want of a better name) the principle of fairness. Suppose we are choosing between two interpretations of a passage. And suppose that on interpretation *A* the passage contains a fallacy, while on interpretation *B* it does not. My principle of fairness requires only this: We should not prefer *A* to *B* unless the balance of textual, contextual, and other evidence favors *A* over *B*. Principles of charity require that we presume, more or less strongly, the absence of a fallacy. The principle of fairness requires only that we *not* presume the *presence* of fallacy. Now even for the principle of fairness, to which I anticipate no objection, it might prove challenging to provide a fully satisfactory theoretical justification. That is a task I will not undertake here.[15]

But an obvious objection is that "the balance of textual, contextual, and other evidence favors A over B" gives us no standard for what is or is not an acceptable interpretation. Quite a lot of evidence would be needed to overcome the presumption that the speaker is reasoning badly when using a weak form of argument.

How does Burke show that this example is not a fallacy? He says the sentence "If capital punishment deterred murder, it would be justified" is not a premise of the argument, but serves only a dialectical function as a prefatory remark.

> Thus viewed, the argument contains one stated premise and this unstated premise: If capital punishment doesn't deter murder, then it isn't justified. The first sentence of the passage, the *stated*

conditional, is not a part of the argument. It has, in addition to any
rhetorical role, the dialectical role of revealing that the arguer accepts
the conclusion *only* because the arguer accepts the stated premise.[16]

So we learn that we can repair an argument of the form "If A, then
B; not A; therefore not B" by ignoring the first premise and adding a
premise "If not A, then not B." That repair works for *any* argument:
If you have premise C and conclusion D, add "If C, then D" and ignore
the other premises. So everyone reasons well all the time.[17]

Example 5 Roofer: I'm positive that my work will meet your requirements.
I really need the money, what with my wife being sick and all.[18]

Analysis Brooke Noel Moore and Richard Parker classify this as
an appeal to pity. "The roofer seems to be giving a reason for thinking
his work will meet your requirements. But of course he is not; that
issue is unaffected by the fact that he really needs the money." Perhaps
by "the issue is unaffected" they mean the argument is weak. That is
so, but it is not enough to classify the argument as a fallacy.

If we accept that the roofer has indeed attempted to make an
argument, we can use the Guide to Repairing Arguments to try to
reconstruct it.

Conclusion: My work will meet your requirements.
Premises: I need the money. My wife is sick.

If we assume the roofer is trying to reason well, an unstated premise is
needed to make the argument valid or strong: "If my wife is sick and I
need the money, then (most probably) my work will meet your requirements." That's implausible. If the roofer seems to be a person who
would not lie nor intentionally mislead, we should assume that he is,
perhaps for the moment, incapable of reasoning well. Or, more likely,
he is not intending to make an argument at all.

To reconstruct what the roofer said as an appeal to pity, we would
need to add the premises: "You should believe that my work will meet
your requirements if you feel sorry for me" and "You should feel sorry
for me if my wife is sick." But there is no reason to think that the
speaker intended or believes those claims; indeed, I've worked with
people who have said something like this who would be seriously
offended were you to say they're asking for your pity. Classifying this
as an appeal to pity violates the Guide to Repairing Arguments: it's
putting words in the speaker's mouth.

Since there is no other substantially different obvious choice for how to repair the argument, it is clear that either the roofer has made a bad argument or no argument at all. But what he has said does not obviously fall into any of the classifications of fallacies given above.

Example 6   The Surgeon General said that smoking is bad for your health. So you should quit smoking.

Analysis   This is an appeal to authority. It requires two unstated premises: "Anything that the Surgeon General says about the health hazards of smoking is (probably) true" and "You should discontinue any habit that is bad for your health."

Both premises are plausible. The Surgeon General is supposed to be an expert on public health matters. It is not a fallacy.

Not every argument of a fallacy type is a bad argument.

Example 7   The Surgeon General said that we should not make marijuana legal. So we should not make marijuana legal.

Analysis   This is an appeal to authority, where the unstated premise that's needed is "What the Surgeon General says about legal matters to do with health issues is (probably) true." Here the premise is dubious: there is no reason to believe that the Surgeon General is an expert on legal, political, or moral matters. This is an appeal to authority that is a fallacy.

Example 8   Zoe: Professor Zzzyzzx gave a talk about writing last night and said the best way to start on a novel is to make an outline of the plot.
        Suzy: Are you kidding? He can hardly speak English.

Analysis   Suzy is trying to convince Zoe that she shouldn't accept the conclusion of Professor Zzzyzzx's argument, using one premise "He can hardly speak English." Her argument requires an unstated premise like, "(Almost) any argument that someone who doesn't speak English well gives about writing a novel is not good." That premise is false. The argument is a fallacy, an example of mistaking the person for the argument.

Compare this to the kind of analysis that van Eemeren and Grootendorst give:

A personal attack on one's opponent is another attempt to eliminate him as a serious partner in the discussion by undermining his right to advance a standpoint or to cast doubt on a standpoint. By portraying

him as stupid, unreliable, inconsistent, or biased, one effectively
silences him, because if the attack is successful he loses his credibility. Strictly speaking, he is not prevented from advancing a standpoint or criticism, but, for practical purposes, he might as well be.
Every attempt to bring about this effect is a violation of Rule 1 and
must be regarded as a fallacy.

Rule 1 for a critical discussion: *Parties must not prevent each other
from advancing standpoints or casting doubt on standpoints.*[19]

By concentrating so much on the rules of the game, van Eemeren
and Grootendorst miss the simple reason for classifying attacks on the
person as fallacies: such an attack usually assumes a claim that is false.
They do not allow for, say, an attack on a person to be a good argument, as when one shows that there is no reason to believe someone's
unsupported premise because he or she is not an expert on that matter.
Their Rule 1 does not tell us when an argument is a fallacy—it is far
too vague for that—but only gives some justification for a classification
already given.

Example 9 Your competitors for law school take Kaplan.

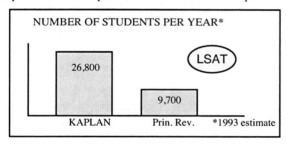

Shouldn't you?
More students trust Kaplan to help them get a higher score because Kaplan
is the undisputed leader in test prep. Find out why. Call today.

   Analysis This advertisement is an attempt to convince, with
unstated conclusion "If you plan to take the Law School Aptitude Test,
you should take Kaplan."

It can be seen as an appeal to fear, requiring: "If you are afraid that
your competitors may gain an advantage by taking Kaplan, then you
should take Kaplan."

Or it can be seen as an appeal to common practice: "If this is the
most popular way to prepare for the LSAT, and you wish to prepare
for the LSAT, then you should take Kaplan."

Either way, the unstated premise is at best dubious, and the argument is a fallacy.

Normally an unstated premise is required to make an argument valid or strong, and the richness of most examples will allow for various choices. The argument is a fallacy only if for each obvious choice of premise(s), the premise is dubious and falls into a type of fallacy. There is no reason to believe that a bad argument can fit into only one type of fallacy.

Conclusion

The usual formulations of what constitutes a fallacy are based on deficient methods of argument analysis. By examining the nature of arguments we can formulate principles for how to repair an argument and when to declare an argument unrepairable. By noting some particular kinds of arguments that are generally not repairable we can shortcut many argument analyses. Each such kind of argument is a fallacy type, and a fallacy is an argument of a fallacy type and which is indeed bad.

NOTES

1. (p. 53) *Fallacies*, p. 12. Some of the criticisms that follow were made by Hamblin.

2. (p. 54) Various modifications of the standard definition have recently been proposed, substituting "sound" or "good" for valid; see Ralph Johnson "The Blaze of Her Splendors" for a survey.

3. (p. 54) "The Pragma-Dialectical Approach to Fallacies", p. 131 and p. 132.

4. (p. 55) Ibid., pp. 133–134.

5. (p. 55) Ibid., p. 136.

6. (p. 55) "The Blaze of Her Splendors."

7. (p. 56) *Attacking Faulty Reasoning*, p. 24.

8. (p. 56) As in T. Edward Damer, *Attacking Faulty Reasoning* and Patrick J. Hurley, *A Concise Introduction to Logic*, p. 160.

9. (p. 57) The term "formal fallacies" is more common than "structural fallacy," but that suggests the argument is invalid according to some formal logic, which may not be the case. Also, "formal fallacy" is used in contrast to "informal fallacy," the division supposedly being exhaustive; Patrick J. Hurley, *A Concise Introduction to Logic*, p. 118, for example, says "Informal fallacies are those that can be detected only through analysis of the content of the argument." He defines content on p. 119 as the meaning of the words in the argument. But for the division to be exhaustive and cover the kinds of fallacies he discusses, the notion of content must also include both false premises and problems that occur in arguments that violate the rules of rational discussion.

10. (p. 59) Some of these names are not standard.

11. (p. 59) This and the next five fallacy types are often classified together as *ad hominem* fallacies.

12. (p. 59) Typically "slippery slope argument" is defined in terms of a causal chain. This definition covers that plus more. Any argument with a chain of conditionals can be suspect. The reason may be due to causal links, to vagueness, or just to each step being a little dubious. Slippery slope arguments are misapplications of a good form of reasoning: transitivity of the conditional.

13. (p. 60) This is not a violation of the rules of rational discussion because sometimes, as in criminal cases in courts, this claim is true.

14. (p. 62) Michael Burke, "Denying the Antecedent: A Common Fallacy?", pp. 23–24.

15. (p. 62) Ibid., pp. 23–24.

16. (p. 63) Ibid., p. 25.

17. (p. 63) One reader suggested that in the context in which the arguer is saying that nothing warrants capital punishment, the example would be a reasonably good argument. But Burke does not suppose that context, and nothing in the example suggests it, other than an unwillingness to classify the argument as bad.

18. (p. 63) Brooke Neal Moore and Richard Parker, *Critical Thinking*, p. 136.

19. (p. 65) *Argumentation, Communication, and Fallacies: A Pragma-Dialectical Perspective*, p. 110 and p. 108. Note that by Rule 1, hitting someone in the midst of a debate would count as a fallacy.

Induction and Deduction

No current definitions of the words "induction" and "deduction" divide arguments according to what we think those words should mean and how we want to use them. Those terms are poor substitutes for a theory of how to evaluate arguments, useful only as a marker for whether we should judge an argument as valid/invalid or on the scale from strong to weak.

The arguer's intention

Patrick J. Hurley makes the following definitions:

> A *deductive* argument is an argument in which the premises are claimed to support the conclusion in such a way that it is *impossible* for the premises to be true and the conclusion false.

> An *inductive* argument is an argument in which the premises are claimed to support the conclusion in such a way that it is *improbable* that the premises be true and the conclusion false.[1]

Max Black says,

> The name "induction" . . . will be used here to cover all cases of nondemonstrative arguments, in which the truth of the premises, while not entailing the truth of the conclusion, purports to be a good reason for belief in it.[2]

Irving M. Copi makes a similar definition:

> We characterize a deductive argument as one whose conclusion is claimed to follow from its premises with absolute necessity, this necessity not being a matter of degree and not depending in any way upon whatever else may be the case. And in sharp contrast we characterize an inductive argument as one whose conclusion is claimed to follow from its premises only with probability, this probability being a matter of degree and dependent upon what else may be the case.[3]

"Claimed" in these definitions shouldn't be understood as meaning explicitly set out in the argument through the use of indicator words. Almost all arguments would fail to be either deductive or inductive in that case.[4] So "claimed" must include implicit claiming. Thus these definitions require us to know the intent of the speaker in order to classify an argument as inductive or deductive or demonstrative (assuming that's what Black means by "purports," since an argument can't purport to do anything). But then there are two problems.

A speaker may be wrong.

> All dogs bark.
> Juney is a dog.
> So it's highly probable that Juney barks.

The premises here are claimed to give only probable but not certain support for the conclusion. So by the definitions above, the argument is inductive. But the words "it's highly probable" are not part of the conclusion of this argument. They indicate the speaker's intent. This is a valid argument, one we typically would classify as deductive.

It may not be clear what the speaker intends.

> Juney barks.
> So Juney is a dog.

Is this deductive or inductive? If the classification is meant to divide all arguments, it must be one or the other. If the speaker is not available, how shall we classify it?

Someone might say the argument lacks a premise. But what premise? There are four obvious choices:

> Juney barks.
> Everything that barks is a dog.
> So Juney is a dog.

> Juney barks.
> Almost everything that barks is a dog.
> So Juney is a dog.

> Juney barks.
> All dogs bark.
> So Juney is a dog.

Juney barks.
Almost all dogs bark.
So Juney is a dog.

Which did the speaker intend? Or did he/she intend any of these? We must make a choice if the classification is to divide all arguments and be of use in analysis.

Deduction as validity

Robert Neidorf avoids intentions in classifying arguments:

> In an inductive argument, the conclusion probably follows from the premises. In a deductive argument, it certainly follows. An argument which fails as deductive may nevertheless constitute a good inductive argument.[5]

These definitions do not divide all arguments into deductive and inductive because weak arguments fit into neither class. For example,

All dogs bark.
Juney barks.
Therefore, Juney is a dog.

This is neither deductive nor inductive, for by this definition there cannot be an invalid deductive argument. If we want to classify this as a bad deductive argument, we shall have to consider the speaker's intention. That is what we do when we invoke the Principle of Rational Discussion and the Guide to Repairing Arguments to classify it as a fallacy.[6] An alternative is to consider all "bad" arguments such as this to be attempts to make strong arguments, as Maurice Finocchiaro does.[7]

Induction as generalization

A different notion of induction classifies an argument as inductive because it generalizes. Carl G. Hempel says:

> The so-called method of inductive inference is usually presented as proceeding from specific cases to a general hypothesis of which each of the special cases is an "instance" in the sense that it conforms to the general hypothesis in question, and thus constitutes confirming evidence for it.[8]

This seems to be a notion of induction as generalization.[9]

Brian Skyrms says:

> *Induction,* (1) in the narrow sense, inference to a generalization from its instances; (2) in the broad sense, any *ampliative inference*—i.e., any inference where the claim made by the conclusion goes beyond the claim jointly made by the premises.[10]

Skyrms' first definition is a clearer version of what Hempel apparently intended. But this doesn't cover cases where we conclude from knowledge from both instances and non-instances, as in the following:

(1) All but one of the dogs I've ever met bark.
     So almost all dogs bark.

> 52% of those polled said they will vote for the incumbent candidate. So 52% of all voters will vote for the incumbent.

Perhaps Skyrms' notion of ampliative inference is meant to include such arguments, but the phrase "goes beyond" is a metaphor not a definition. If taken seriously, any invalid argument would be an ampliative inference since the conclusion goes beyond the premises— that's why it's invalid.

Similarly, Nicholas Rescher says:

> Dictionaries sometimes define induction as "inference to a general conclusion from particular cases." But such inferences—e.g., from "spaniels eat meat," "schnauzers eat meat," "corgis eat meat," etc., to "all dogs eat meat"—illustrate only one particular kind of inductive reasoning. Nor will it do to add merely those inferences to a particular conclusion that move from effects to causes—from the smoke to the fire, or from the bark to the dog. For this does not go far enough. Inference from sample to population and its inverse, from part to whole (from the jaws to the entire alligator), from style to authorship, from clue to culprit, from symptom to disease, etc., are all also modes of inductive inference. The crucial thing about induction is its movement beyond the evidence in hand—from informatively lesser data to relatively larger conclusions.[11]

John Stuart Mill offers not one but four definitions or conditions for induction:

> For the purposes of the present inquiry, Induction may be defined, the operation of discovering and proving general propositions.

> Induction, then, is that operation of the mind, by which we infer that what we know to be true in a particular case or cases, will be true in

all cases which resemble the former in certain assignable respects. In other words, Induction is the process by which we conclude that what is true of certain individuals of a class is true of the whole class, or that what is true at certain times will be true in similar circumstances at all times. ...

Induction, as above defined, is a process of inference; it proceeds from the known to the unknown.[12]

But these definitions don't seem to cover the arguments at (1) above.

Deduction and formal logic

Formal logic alone cannot determine what is deductive. It is normally our judgment of whether an argument is valid that determines how we formalize it in a formal logic, rather than vice-versa. Consider:

(2) Juney is a black dog.
     So Juney is a dog.

This is said to be valid because it is classified so in predicate logic. We rewrite it as:

(3) Juney is black and Juney is a dog.
     So Juney is a dog.

But to do so, we must informally recognize that the following is valid:

Juney is a black dog.
Therefore, Juney is black and Juney is a dog.

This is what justifies (2) as valid and what justifies our rewriting (2) as (3). Compare:

Juney is a toy dog.
So Juney is a dog.

This is not valid, though it has the same form as (2). We know it is not valid because we know what "toy dog" means.

Deductive arguments cannot be identified as those that are classi-fied by their form only as valid by (some) formal logic.

Conclusion

The terms "induction" and "deduction," though widely used in the analysis of arguments, give no clear standard of evaluation.

NOTES

1. (p. 69) *A Concise Introduction to Logic*.

2. (p. 69) "Induction," p. 169.

3. (p. 69) *Introduction to Logic*, p. 26.

4. (p. 70) See the hundreds of examples in *Critical Thinking*.

5. (p. 71) *Deductive Forms*. In *Logic and Contemporary Rhetoric*, p. 10, Howard Kahane tries to avoid the issue by defining only "deductively valid" and "inductively valid" arguments.

6. (p. 71) See "Arguments" and "Fallacies" in this volume.

7. (p. 71) See p. 32 of "Arguments" in this volume.

8. (p. 71) "Studies in the Logic of Confirmation," p. 5.

9. (p. 71) Hempel was concerned with induction in explanations, not arguments. But the issues are the same, as explained in "Explanations" in *Cause and Effect, Conditionals, Explanations* in this series of books and in "Generalizing" in this volume.

10. (p. 72) "Induction." Compare L. Jonathan Cohen, *The Philosophy of Induction and Probability*, p. 1: "Induction is termed 'ampliative' when it extrapolates beyond the existing data."

11. (p. 72) *Induction*, p. 7. This is the only place Rescher defines "induction" in that book. Note that "spaniels eat meat" is not a particular instance of "all dogs eat meat" but is itself a generalization.

12. (p. 73) *A System of Logic*, Book III, Chapter I, section 2, p. 208 and III.II.1, p. 210.

Base Claims

Unless we accept some claims without reasoning to them, we can have no good reason to believe any claim. In this paper we'll consider what counts as good reason to believe a claim without reasoning.

A claim we have good reason to believe may be plausible to us.

Plausible claims A claim is *plausible* to a particular person at a particular time if:

- The person has good reason to believe it.
- The person recognizes that he or she has good reason to believe it.
- The person believes it.

Plausibility is not an either-or classification. We have an informal scale for each of the conditions, from better reason to believe to worse reason to believe, from recognizing clearly to being oblivious, from believing strongly to strongly disbelieving. Combined, we have an informal scale from the least plausible to the most implausible.

The question, then, is what counts as good reason to believe a claim. Sometimes we can and do reason to a claim being true, and when we do so we are making an argument.

Arguments An *argument* is an attempt to convince someone (possibly yourself) that a particular claim called the ***conclusion*** is true. The rest of the argument is a collection of claims called ***premises*** which are given as reasons for believing the conclusion is true.

Good arguments An argument is *good* if and only if it gives good reason to believe its conclusion.

The following are necessary conditions for an argument to be good:

- The premises are plausible.
- The premises are more plausible than the conclusion.
- The argument is valid or strong.

Whether these conditions are sufficient for an argument to be good is a question that is discussed throughout the essays in this volume. In practice, we usually do consider them to be sufficient.

Since both the plausibility of the premises and the strength of an argument are relative to a particular person at a particular time, whether an argument is good depends on the person to whom the argument is addressed, though in practice we can usually agree on our evaluations.

If we recognize that an argument is good, then the canons of good reasoning enjoin that we should believe its conclusion, as discussed in "Rationality" in this volume.

But unless we accept some claims as plausible without reasoning to them, we can have no good reason to believe any claim: Every argument depends on taking some claims as plausible, and we would be faced with an infinite regress. In this paper we'll consider what counts as good reason to believe a claim without reasoning to it.

Example 1   The President of the United States was born in the United States.

Analysis   We have good reason to believe this claim. So we do not have good reason to believe "The President of the United States was born in Kenya." They can't both be true, though both could be false.

Contrary and contradictory claims   Two claims are *contrary* if it's not possible for both of them to be true at the same time in the same way. Two claims are *contradictory* if any way the one could be true the other is false.

Note that contradictory claims are also contrary.

If we were to have good reason to believe both a claim and a contrary of it, we'd have good reason to believe both that the claim is true and that it is false. Whatever we mean by "good reason to believe a claim," it can't include that.[1]

Good reason and contrary claims   If you have good reason to believe a claim, then you do not have good reason to believe a contrary of it.

Example 2   Wanda: I've had these goldfish for three years and
             they've never had any babies. Why is that?

Dick: Did you get them at a pet store?

Wanda: Yes.

Dick: Well, all goldfish you buy at a pet store are male.

Analysis Wanda really doubts that what Dick has said is true. But she realizes she's got no better reason to think that some of the goldfish sold at pet stores are female. So she should suspend judgment on which of these claims is true.

Suspending judgment If you do not have substantially better reason to believe a claim than to believe a contrary of it, then you do not have good reason to believe either claim. In that case you should suspend judgment on whether it is true.

Let's pick out those claims for which reasoning does not supply us with good reason to believe are true or are false.[2]

Base claims A claim is *base* for a particular person at a particular time if and only if there is no good argument he or she is aware of that has it or a contrary of it as conclusion.

Example 3 Spot is a dog.

Analysis Tom has seen Dick's dog Spot. He's sure that no argument can give him better reason to believe this claim more than just seeing Spot. So it's a base claim for him. But to Rudolfo, who overhears Tom talking about Spot and infers from the conversation that Spot is a dog, the example is not a base claim.

Example 4 God exists.

Analysis Harry is an agnostic. He can find no good argument for this claim, nor can he find a good argument for "God does not exist." Nor does he have any special insight that tells him that either of these are true. So he suspends judgment on both. Thus, both "God exists" and "God does not exist" are base for him. Any claim for which someone has good reason to suspend judgment is base for that person.

Harry has seen arguments for this claim which he recognizes are valid inferences. Each, though, has at least one premise that is not more plausible to him than "God exists." A person can infer a base claim from other claims, even from other base claims. But such an inference cannot give him or her good reason to believe the claim more than without the inference unless the premises are more plausible than the conclusion.

Example 5   Fred Kroon is in New Zealand.

Analysis   For Fred Kroon and anyone else who happens to be around him, this is a base claim. He and they may, if they wish, reason to its truth, citing that they know the place they are in is New Zealand, citing further evidence for that, and that they know that this is Fred Kroon, citing further evidence for that. But they need not. After all, eventually they will reach a place in their justification of why they believe the claim that cannot be justified by reasoning. And for some, it might as well be at that claim itself.

However, someone who calls Fred Kroon on the telephone, dialing a number in New Zealand, can reason to the truth of the claim, not deeming it a base claim.

Example 6   This is a rock.

Analysis   Normally most of us would take this as a base claim. But an elderly woman who knows her eyesight is failing and her sense of touch isn't sure enough to distinguish whether what she's picked up is a rock or a fragment of concrete might enlist the aid of others to tell her and then reason from that to whether the claim is true or false.

Example 7   Dick: Hey Zoe, look, our neighbor's house is white.

Analysis   Dick said this while looking at his neighbor's house that used to be brown. He thinks that there's no evidence he could imagine that would convince him more than just seeing the house. But then Zoe asks him how he knows the rest of the house and not just the side facing him is white. Dick realizes he's just assumed that, though he can see now how to give a good argument for it. So what he took to be a base claim is no longer base for him.

We have seen in these examples that:

- Any claim for which someone has good reason to suspend judgment is base for that person.

- If a claim is base for a person at a particular time, then any contrary of it is base for him or her, too.

- What is a base claim for one person need not be a base claim for another.

- What is a base claim depends on our experience, our knowledge, and our perceptual abilities.

- What is a base claim for a person at one time may not be base for that same person at a later time.

Example 8 Suzy: Dr. E isn't married.

Analysis Suzy takes this as a base claim. But that's only because she hasn't thought about it very much and can't recognize a good argument when she sees one. That a claim is base for Suzy at a particular time is a weak condition and says more about her beliefs and ability to reason than about reasons she has to believe the claim. We need a stronger standard.

Properly base claims A claim is *properly base* for a particular person at a particular time if and only if it is both base and plausible for that person.

If a claim is properly base for a person, then he or she has good reason to believe it, but that reason isn't and can't be from reasoning for that person at that time.

Example 9 Alvin Plantinga: God exists.

Analysis Plantinga says in "Is Belief in God Properly Basic?" that this is a properly base claim for him. Hence, "God does not exist" is not properly base for him. Nonetheless, "God does not exist" is base for him.[3]

Example 10 Early morning—barely awakening I hear a cock crow, then another crows. I know:

This is the crow of a cock.
There are two cocks.
One is close to my bedroom window and one is farther away.

I know these. They are base claims for me.

Analysis I can justify my belief in these claims with an argument, convincing you that they are true if you believe my reports on the kind of sounds I heard (loud, soft, one in response to the other, . . .). But such reasoning doesn't change that they are base claims for me. I am built to make such judgments accurately, though I can be wrong. It is not an argument that makes them believable to me but the normal workings of my body that processes such sounds. That those processes can be investigated and challenged does not make the claims less base at the time I make the judgment.

Example 11 This is a banana.

Analysis To many of us, claims such as "This is a banana" and "This is solid" are base claims, and whenever we recognize that they are true they are properly base. We can use definitions to lead someone to see that they are true, but we can't reason to them. Asserting "This is solid" is no more than pointing to the object and saying "Solid" and perhaps knocking on it. In that situation knowing what the word means we know that the claim is true, and there's no claim more plausible to us from which we can infer it.

But Eloise, who's been studying philosophy, says that "This is a banana" is not base to her. She says she can infer it from more plausible claims:

This looks like a banana.
I have no reason to think that my senses are deceiving me now.
Therefore, this is a banana.

But this argument lacks at least one premise:

If my senses are not deceiving me, and this appears to be a banana, then this is a banana.

It's hard to imagine that Eloise finds this to be more plausible than "This is a banana." Perhaps she does. Then, unlike most of us, she doesn't take "This is a banana" to be base.

Example 12 Dick: I'm cold right now.

Analysis Dick knows this claim to be true or false by intro-spection. It's a properly base claim for him. But for Zoe this isn't a base claim. She can determine its truth or falsity only by evidence —behavioral evidence—that she accumulates and then applies in reasoning. What is base depends on our perspective.

Example 13 Dick: That's a plant.

Analysis Dick said this when he went to his dentist's office and saw a plant in a vase. He believed the claim, and he had good reason to believe it, for he was looking at the plant. The claim was, at that time, a properly base claim for him. But he was wrong: it was an artificial plant. Good reason to believe a claim need not be perfect reason to believe it. A claim that is properly base for a person need not be true.

Perhaps we could define a "perfect base claim" for a person to be a base claim that he or she has perfect reason to believe. Then every perfect base claim is true. But not every true properly base claim would necessarily be a perfect base claim, as the next example illustrates.

Example 14   Tom: This is a dog.

Analysis   Tom said this while stroking Luigi's pet. It was a properly base claim for him at that time. Harry looks at Luigi's pet and thinks it's a wolf hybrid. He challenges Tom, and Tom realizes that he doesn't have perfect reason to believe the claim. But really Tom is right and Harry is wrong.

Perhaps Tom could do a DNA test in order to get perfect reason to believe "This is a dog." But then that claim wouldn't be base for him because he could formulate the evidence he has for it in terms of claims about DNA and doghoodity.

Tom can't formulate in terms of claims the evidence he has from seeing the animal. If he could, then "This is a dog" wouldn't be base for him. And if we could do that generally, there would be no base claims, and hence no good arguments, for we'd never have non-propositional evidence, and so no place from which to start our reasoning.

Classifying claims as perfect base would be of little use to us in evaluating reasoning, for we would have to be able to recognize perfect evidence as perfect without argument in order to take a claim to be a perfect base claim and hence suitable to use as a premise. That is too high a standard for using arguments to arrive at what we hope are truths.

We have seen in these examples that:

- Someone when challenged may be able to provide an argument for a claim that he or she takes as base, but that need not make the claim more secure knowledge for him or her, nor need it mean that the claim was not base when first evaluated.

- What we take as base may depend on how much we are willing to rely on our senses for evidence.

- What is properly base for one person may not even be base for another.

- A claim that is properly base for a person may nonetheless be false.

- A claim may be properly base for a person, and it may be true, yet the person might not have "perfect" reason to believe it.

Example 15 7 is a thing

Analysis A platonist says that this is true and no reasoning can determine that. However, a nominalist argues by reasoning that it is false. Similarly, "The concept of man is a universal," "What is red is not white," and "This is a dog" (said while pointing to something) are or are not base claims depending on the metaphysics we accept.

We might say that both "The earth revolves around the sun" and "Richard L. Epstein lives in New Mexico" are true if and only if they describe how the world is, but that conceals the metaphysics we take as the grounds for each to be true. The empiricist and the idealist reason together under the rubric "What is true is what corresponds to the case" while differing greatly on what constitutes corresponding to the case.

Example 16 There are things in the world.

Analysis We take "This is a thing" to be a properly base claim when we're pointing to a dog. We take "This is a thing" to be a properly base claim when we're pointing to a banana. From many examples such as these, we deduce "There are things in the world." So the example is not a base claim.[4]

That's wrong.

For those of us who believe the example is true, it is a properly base claim. No examples lead to it. We believe it because it's part of the way we see the world through the grammar of our language: we learn with our language that there are things in the world. Someone can be an empiricist, can believe in an external world, and yet not believe this example if raised to speak a process language, one whose grammar codifies a view of the world as process and not as made up of things.[5] If the person speaks English as well as that other language, he or she might say, "Perhaps to you it seems there are things, but though I can speak your language, I do not think there are."[6]

For those of us who speak English and believe this example, it is a properly base claim. But so, too, is "This is a thing" when pointing to a dog. Neither can serve as a premise for the other in a good argument

because neither is more plausible than the other. A base claim need not
be a simple claim.

Example 17   Alvin Plantinga says:

> A second objection I've often heard: if belief in God is properly
> basic, why can't *just any* belief be properly basic? Couldn't we say
> the same for any bizarre aberration we can think of? What about
> voodoo or astrology? What about the belief that the Great Pumpkin
> returns every Halloween? Could I properly take *that* as basic? And
> if I can't, why can I properly take belief in God as basic? Suppose I
> believe that if I flap my arms with sufficient vigor, I can take off and
> fly about the room; could I defend myself against the charge of
> irrationality by claiming this belief is basic? If we say that belief in
> God is properly basic, won't we be committed to holding that just
> anything, or nearly anything, can properly be taken as basic, thus
> throwing wide the gates to irrationalism and superstition?[7]

Analysis   People have taken a great deal as properly base in the
past, and they do so now. They take many claims to be true without
proof which to most of us seem silly, superstitious, or just plain false.
But those people are irrational only if they persist in their belief in the
face of a good argument for a contrary that they recognize as a good
argument.[8] That's what distinguishes belief in evolution from belief in
the creation of the world 5,000 years ago. But not entirely, because
those who hold that latter belief do not accept that we have given a
good argument against it. So they are not irrational. They just can't
reason well, or are unwilling to reason well—by our standards.
Similarly for "God exists": there's no good argument against it, nor is
there a good argument for it. But the lack of a good argument for a
claim does not mean that belief in the claim is irrational. Someone can
accept "God exists" as a properly base claim taking as evidence some
ineffable revelation.

What we take as a properly base claim depends on our metaphysics, often codified in our language, whether that is made explicit
or not. But more, what we take as properly base is often an expression
of our metaphysics.

With our fundamental metaphysical assumptions come standards
or criteria for what counts as a good reason to believe a claim without
an argument. An empiricist might say that seeing is believing; a
platonist might say intellectual perception. Or a devout Christian might

say revelation by God; a Muslim, revelation by Allah; a believer in the faith of Dog, the barking of Dog to him. But even those could be formulated as claims, such as "Dog told me that Luigi's pet is a dog." Rather, it is the feeling, a revelation through mind and body independent of any way to put that into words as a claim, that is the good reason to believe such a claim, those people might say. Given our background in speaking English, most of us would say that good reason to believe "This is a dog" is seeing the dog.

It is a mistake to ask whether we have good reason to believe the claims of our metaphysics. They are what gives us, in part, good reason to believe any other claim. To doubt that we have good reason to believe one of them is to embark on a project to construct another metaphysics or to go down the path of the Pyrrhonian skeptic way, not an impetus to look for a good argument for it.[9] Whatever reasons we have for believing a claim of our metaphysics count as good reason to believe it. That is the start of any analysis of how to reason well. We can disagree with someone else's metaphysics; we can say that their assumptions are wrong; we can say that they are violating the canons of good reasoning—according to our standards of what is good reasoning. But unless there are standards independent of all metaphysics by which we can judge metaphysics, we cannot show another's metaphysics to be false except by recourse to our own metaphysics, which that person would not accept. We can only lead another through pointing, talking, ritual, or some other means to see the world as we do.[10]

We have seen in these examples that:

- What is a base claim for a person depends on the metaphysics he or she accepts.

- A base claim may depend on the grammar of our language.

- A base claim need not be a simple claim nor a claim about a particular thing or part of the world.

- A person might take as properly base a claim that we consider bizarre, yet we may have no clear justification for calling his or her belief irrational.

- Claims that are part of or express part of our metaphysics are properly base claims for us.

These observations give us some idea of what is a base claim and what counts as good reason to believe a base claim. As well, we have the constraints imposed on what counts as good reason to believe given by the principles of suspending judgment and of good reason and contrary claims. But what counts as good reason to believe a base claim must also include a particular view of truth and what things are true or false.[11] Given those constraints, we can develop criteria for what counts as good reason to believe an unsupported claim relative to our metaphysics, as I have done in the textbook *Critical Thinking*.

NOTES

1. (p. 76) See "Truth and Reasoning" in *Prescriptive Reasoning* in this volume for a discussion of this.

2. (p. 77) The definition of base claim and of properly base claim here are motivated by the definitions given by Alvin Plantinga in "Is Belief in God Properly Basic?" but they are not the same as his.

3. (p. 79) According to our definitions.

4. (p. 82) Compare Alvin Plantinga in "Is Belief in God Properly Basic?":

> It is relatively specific and concrete propositions rather than their more general and abstract colleagues that are properly basic. Perhaps such items are
>
>> There are trees.
>> There are other persons,
>
> and The world has existed for more than 5 minutes,
>
> are not properly basic; it is instead such propositions as
>
>> I see a tree,
>> that person is pleased,
>
> and I had breakfast more than an hour ago
>
> that deserve that accolade. Of course propositions of the latter sort immediately and self-evidently entail propositions of the former sort; and perhaps there is thus no harm in speaking of the former as properly basic, even though so to speak is to speak a bit loosely. p. 47

5. (p. 82) See my essay "The World as Process" in *Reasoning and Formal Logic* in this series of books.

6. (p. 82) Compare the constructivist mathematician who is asked to teach a course on set theory. He can speak that language of infinities and teach students but still find it to be inherently incomprehensible, as I have done.

7. (p. 83) "Is Belief in God Properly Basic?", p. 48. In that paper Plantinga is not entirely clear what he means by "properly basic": whether it is what I call "base" or what I call "properly base."

8. (p. 83) As discussed in "Rationality."

9. (p. 84) See *The Skeptic Way: Sextus Empiricus' Outlines of Pyrrhonism* by Benson Mates.

10. (p. 84) Compare "The World as Process."

11. (p. 84) See "Reasoning and Truth" in *Prescriptive Reasoning*.

Analogies

An analogy elevates a comparison into an argument, reasoning from similarities to similar conclusions. Some examples will show that analogies are often incomplete arguments. A general method is suggested for how to evaluate and repair analogies.

What is an analogy?
An analogy is a kind of argument.

Reasoning by analogy A comparison becomes reasoning by analogy when a claim is being argued for: on one side of the comparison we draw a conclusion, so on the other side we should draw a similar one.

What do we mean by "similar conclusion"? I won't try to make that precise. Rather, I'll present some examples that show how we can evaluate analogies, which will give us some guide for how to proceed in reasoning by analogy.

Example 1 Country Joe McDonald was a well-known singer who wrote songs protesting the war in Vietnam. In 1995 he was interviewed on National Public Radio about his motives for working to establish a memorial for Vietnam War soldiers in Berkeley, California, his home and the center for anti-war protests in the 1960s and 1970s. He said:

Blaming soldiers for war is like blaming firemen for fires.

Analysis This is a comparison. But it's meant as an argument:

We don't blame firemen for fires.
Firemen and fires are like soldiers and wars.
Therefore, we should not blame soldiers for war.

This sounds pretty reasonable. But something's missing. In what way are firemen and fires like soldiers and wars? They have to be similar

enough in some respect for Country Joe's remark to be more than
suggestive.

Both firemen and soldiers:

wear uniforms
answer to a chain of command
cannot disobey a superior without serious consequences
fight fires/wars that are dangerous for others if left unfought
have their work done when the fire/war is over
until recently were only men
put their lives at risk in work
firemen don't start fires—soldiers don't start wars
usually drink beer

That's stupid: Firemen and soldiers usually drink beer.

It's not just any similarity that's important. There must be some
crucial, important way that firemen fighting fires is like soldiers fighting wars, some similarity that can account for why we don't blame
firemen for fires that also applies to soldiers and war. Some of these
similarities don't seem to matter. Others we can't use because they
trade on an ambiguity, like saying firemen "fight" fires.

We don't have any good guide for how to proceed—that's a
weakness of the original argument. But if we're to take Country Joe
McDonald's remark seriously, we have to come up with some principle
that applies to both sides.

The similarity that seems most important is that both firemen and
soldiers are involved in dangerous work, trying to end a problem/
disaster they didn't start. And we don't want to blame someone for
helping to end a disaster that could harm us all.

Picking out the relevant similarities amounts to making the vague
sentence "Firemen and fires are like soldiers and wars" into premises:

(1) Firemen are involved in dangerous work.
     Soldiers are involved in dangerous work.
     The job of a fireman is to end a fire.
     The job of a soldier is to end a war.
     Firemen don't start fires.
     Soldiers don't start wars.

These are the similarities. Still, added to the original argument, we
don't get the conclusion that we shouldn't blame soldiers for wars.
We need a general principle:

You shouldn't blame someone for helping to end a disaster, if
he or she didn't start the disaster.

Then we have a valid argument. And this principle is plausible.

But is the argument good? Are all the premises true? This is the
point where the differences between firemen and soldiers might be
important.

The first two premises of (1) are clearly true. As is the third.

But is the job of soldiers to end a war? And do soldiers really not
start wars? Look at this difference:

Without firemen there would still be fires.
Without soldiers there wouldn't be any wars.

Yes, there would still be violence. But without soldiers—any soldiers
anywhere—there could be no organized violence of one country against
another.

So? The analogy shouldn't convince. The argument has a dubious
premise.

Perhaps the premises at (1) could be modified, using that soldiers
are usually drafted. But that's beyond Country Joe's argument. If he
meant something deeper, then it's his responsibility to flesh it out. Or
we could use his comparison as a springboard to decide whether there
is some other general principle, based on the similarities, for why we
shouldn't blame soldiers for war.

Example 2 Magic Johnson was allowed to play in the National
Basketball Association, and he was HIV-positive. So people who
are HIV-positive should be allowed to remain in the military.

Analysis This doesn't seem very convincing. What has the NBA
to do with the military? We can list similarities (uniforms, teamwork,
orders, winning, penalties for disobeying orders) and differences (great
pay/lousy pay, voluntary/involuntary, game/not a game), but none of
these matter unless we hit on the basis of the argument.

The only reason for eliminating someone from a job who is
    HIV-positive is the risk of contracting AIDS for others
    who work with that person.
Magic Johnson was allowed to play basketball when he was
    HIV-positive.
So in basketball the risk of contracting AIDS from a fellow
    worker is considered insignificant.

> Basketball players have as much chance of physical contact
>   and contracting AIDS from one another as soldiers do
>   (except in war).
> Therefore, the risk of contracting AIDS from a fellow soldier
>   should be considered insignificant.
> Therefore, people who are HIV positive should be allowed to
>   remain in the military.

Here it is not the similarities between basketball players and soldiers that are important. Once we spot the general principle (the first premise), it is the differences that support the conclusion (basketball players sweat and bleed on one another every day, soldiers normally do not, except in war). Whether the analogy is good depends on whether these premises are true, but it's certainly better than it seemed at first glance.

Example 3 You should treat dogs humanely. How would you feel if you were caged up all day and experimented on? Or if you were chained to a stake all day? Or someone beat you every time you did something wrong?

Analysis We can take each of the questions as rhetorical and get an argument by analogy. The unstated claim is that dogs are like humans.

> It would be morally unacceptable to cage up and experiment
>   on a human.
> It would be morally unacceptable to chain a human to a stake
>   all day.
> It would be morally unacceptable to beat a human every time
>   he/she did something wrong.
> Dogs are like humans.
> Therefore, it is morally unacceptable to do any of these
>   things to a dog. That is, you should treat dogs humanely.

Is the argument good? We have to replace the vague sentence "Dogs are like humans" with specific ways in which dogs and humans are similar, and then devise a general principle that applies to both dogs and humans.

The fundamental similarity of dogs to humans is that they are both mammals. We can use that similarity to flesh out the argument by adding as premises:

Dogs are mammals.
Humans are mammals.
You should treat mammals humanely.

This would do, though the general claim is too broad to be plausible to many of us, since it covers cats. The only other clue we have to the speaker's intent is that she says, "How would you feel . . ." She believes that we can imagine what it would be like to be a dog treated badly. We could flesh out the analogy, then, with premises:

You can imagine what it would be like to be another person treated badly.
You can imagine what it would be like to be a dog treated badly.
You should treat humanely any creature that you can imagine what it would feel like to be mistreated.

This might be better, for it would justify some people treating fish humanely, while others would reject that since they can't imagine what a fish feels.

Which is the better analysis of the original analogy? Both are reasonable interpretations. But both need to be improved considerably before they would be good arguments. As is often the case with an analogy, a comparison and a conclusion are just a starting place for a serious discussion of an issue, for attempts to find principles that we all find plausible.

Example 4 I have certain physical attributes: $X, Y, Z, \ldots$ (being descriptions of my muscles and nerves and brain). These attributes are connected, according to the best biological theories and evidence we currently have, to my having sensations of pain in the presence of particular stimuli such as $A, B, C, \ldots$. You have the same physical attributes in the sense of the same construction, though not identical. I feel pain when subjected to those stimuli. Therefore, you feel pain, too, when subjected to those stimuli.

Analysis Something like this is the argument by similar construction for others feeling pain.

Here the similarities are made explicit. But after listing each of the premises we can ask, "So?" We can list lots of possibilities of how the premises could be true and conclusion false: you feel something, but it's not at all like the pain I feel; you are an automaton; it is the precise construction and not a similar one that results in my feeling pain; . . . .

The proponent of the argument might say that these are all unlikely, so the argument is strong. But to show that these are indeed unlikely, that person should be able to produce a plausible claim that rules them out (this is the principle that an argument is not strong by default which is presented in "Arguments" in this volume). The only candidate I can see is: These attributes are causally sufficient for someone feeling pain under these stimuli. But to add that would beg the question. So the argument is not good, and there's no obvious repair.[1]

Analogies and the common law

One place where analogies are analyzed carefully, with the relevant similarities pointed out and a general principle stated, is in common law. Edward H. Levi, *An Introduction to Legal Reasoning*, says:

> The basic pattern of legal reasoning is reasoning by example. It is reasoning from case to case. It is a three-step process described by the doctrine of precedent in which a proposition descriptive of the first case is made into a rule of law and then applied to a next similar situation. The steps are these: similarity is seen between cases; next the rule of law inherent in the first case is announced; then the rule of law is made applicable to the second case. pp. 1–2

Laws as written are often vague, or situations come up which no one ever imagined might be covered by the law: Do the liability decisions applying to horses and carriages apply to cars, too? Similarities or differences have to be pointed out, general principles enunciated. Then those principles have to be respected by other judges. That's the idea of precedent in common law.

Why should judges respect how earlier ones ruled? If there is no consistency in the application of the law, then we cannot predict if our actions will be criminal and/ or open to civil penalties. We cannot plan and act. To be a society governed by laws, the laws must be applied consistently: unpredictability can paralyze a society.

Only a few times has the Supreme Court of the United States said that all the rulings on one issue, including rulings the Supreme Court made, are completely wrong. *Brown v. the Board of Education* said that segregation in schools, which had been ruled legal for nearly a hundred years, was now illegal. *Roe v. Wade* said that having an abortion, which had been ruled illegal for more than a century, was now legal. Such decisions are rare. They have to be. They create immense turmoil in the ways we live. We have to rethink a lot. And we can't do that regularly.

So what does a judge do when she is confronted by fifteen cases that were decided one way, the case before her falls under the general principle that was stated to cover those cases, yet justice demands that she decide this case the other way? She looks for differences between this case and those fifteen others. She tweaks the general principle just enough to get another principle that covers all those fifteen cases, but doesn't include the one she's deciding. She makes a new decision that now must be respected or overthrown.

Analogies and generalizations

Example 5   Zoe has a Plymouth Voyager, and she's had a lot of problems with the doors not fitting properly. Wanda has one, too, and has the same problem. So if you buy a Voyager, you'll probably find that you'll have the same problem with the doors.

Analysis   Some say this is a different kind of argument, not from a claim about some to a claim about more, but directly from particulars to particulars.[2] If so, we need criteria by which to evaluate such an argument. But the criteria are obvious:

> The particulars in the premises must be sufficient to establish a
> general claim by a generalization. From that general claim
> and a description of the particular in the conclusion, we should
> get a good argument.

In this case we would have:

> Zoe has a Plymouth Voyager, and she's had a lot of problems
>   with the doors not fitting properly.
> Wanda has a Plymouth Voyager, and she has had a lot of
>   problems with the doors not fitting properly.
> Therefore, almost all Plymouth Voyagers have problems
>   with their doors not fitting properly.

> Almost all Plymouth Voyagers have problems with their doors
>   not fitting properly.
> Therefore, any Plymouth Voyager you plan to buy will have
>   problems with its doors not fitting properly.

This reconstruction isolates the weakness of the argument: the sample is too small and we've no reason to believe the sample is representative.

Analogies from particulars to particulars can be rewritten according to our general rules for argument repair as set out in "Arguments" in this volume. They require a generalization and an application of the generalization. They are not a new form of argument, but a condensed form of two kinds of arguments for which we already have established methods of analysis.

Some analogies (though hardly all, as some of the examples above illustrate) require generalizations to be fleshed out into good arguments. But every analogy requires some general principle to be good. J. M. Keynes tried to make precise the nature of the similarity in an analogy by saying that both objects satisfy the same propositional function.[3] But analogies are not always about objects: in Example 1 it is the relationship between firemen and fires that is being compared to the relationship between soldiers and wars.

Conclusion

Though there seems to be little we can provide as a general guide for analyzing analogies, there is enough to show us a direction for analysis. Analogies, though usually only sketches for arguments, are nonetheless part of the general method we use in all our reasoning: consider two or more situations, or things, or masses, or relations, or processes to be similar and generalize or draw similar conclusions. The general claims that justify such reasoning may be about the nature of reasoning or particular to the argument at hand. In the end, we recognize, or see, or perhaps just agree on similarities, abstract from those, and justify our reasoning. Analogies are the basis, if a very informal basis, the first step in seeing how we can do that.

NOTES

1. (p. 92) A fuller analysis of this argument is given in "Subjective Claims" in this volume.

2. (p. 93) See *Definition and Induction: A Historical and Comparative Study* by Kisor Kumar Chakrabarti for a discussion of this view in classical Indian philosophy.

3. (p. 94) *A Treatise on Probability*, pp. 222–223.

Subjective Claims

with

Fred Kroon and William S. Robinson

We reason about the world around us. We reason about our thoughts and feelings and the thoughts and feelings of others.

We need to have a basis for distinguishing claims about these apparently different subjects in order to investigate how we do or should reason with them. After surveying ways to characterize those, we'll propose a definition of "subjective claim" and look at examples of classifying according to it. Then we'll turn to what role this division plays in our reasoning and what consequences that has on whether we can provide a bridge through reasoning between the mental and the non-mental in our lives.

Some current definitions of "subjective"
We are concerned here with how to reason about the mental life of creatures and things. The reasoning we're concerned with can be shared among us using language.

Claims A claim is a written or uttered piece of language that we agree to view as being either true or false but not both.

The word "uttered" is meant to include silent uttering to oneself, what we might call "thinking" some word or phrase. The nature of claims is discussed further in "Arguments" in this volume.

People have been using the terms "subjective" and "objective" in talking about questions of mind and the world external to us. But often it is not clear what they mean by those terms.[1] Here are some definitions that have been proposed or are in use now.

• *Definition 1*   A claim is subjective if and only if it is about at least one subject.

Here "a subject" is to be understood as something that has a mental life.

Example 1   Wanda weighs more than 110 kgs.

Analysis   By Definition 1 this is a subjective claim: We all believe and have as standard background that human beings are subjects. But the example is not about the mental state of any creature, and we suspect that most of us are inclined to classify this as objective. Using this definition, any claim about a person would be subjective.

Example 2   This starfish is afraid of being touched.

Analysis   To classify this as subjective or objective by this definition we need to decide whether a starfish is a subject. But it is the evaluation of claims such as this that will lead us to decide whether we should believe a starfish is capable of feelings or thoughts. The evaluation of this claim would seem to depend on the same kinds of evidence and methods of reasoning we would use to determine whether "Bill is afraid of dogs" is true.

This definition doesn't classify claims in accord with the distinction of claims about mental lives versus claims about an external world. Worse, it requires us to have a clear analysis of what is a subject and hence of consciousness before we can apply it, so that it will not be an aid in investigating how to reason about consciousness.

• *Definition 2*   A claim is subjective if and only if there could be two subjects who are not known to be deficient in their epistemic responsibilities and who disagree regarding the truth-value of the claim.

Variations on this definition replace "not known to be deficient in their epistemic responsibilities" with "are rational," or "are justified in their beliefs," or a similar phrase.[2]

Example 3 There is enough oil available in the world for extraction by current means to fulfill the current level of consumption for the next forty years.

Analysis This claim is subjective by Definition 2. But there's nothing about subjects or consciousness that is at stake in deciding the truth-value of it.

Example 4 Spot is in pain.

Analysis Seeing Dick's dog Spot whining after being bitten by a cat, licking his paw and limping, we'd all agree that this claim is true. Hence, it would be objective by Definition 2. Yet it is clearly meant to be about the mental life of some creature.

Any claim that is debatable is subjective by Definition 2 but becomes objective once we get more or less universal agreement about its truth-value. Invoking what a "rational person" believes cannot resolve that problem because there is little agreement as to what constitutes a rational person (see "Rationality" in this volume) and, worse, to make the notion of rationality clear we need to understand what counts as good reasoning, which includes reasoning with claims about the mental life of others.

An important distinction can be made between a claim being about the mental life of some creature and whose truth-value almost everyone agrees on and a claim that is not about the mental life of anything. But we cannot consider that distinction if we use a definition that conflates those.

• *Definition 3* C. E. M. Joad says:

> A subjective judgement we will define as a judgement to the effect that the experience of the person making the judgement is being modified in a certain way—in other words, that something is happening in or to "the subject." An objective judgement we will define as a judgement to the effect that the world external to the person judging is characterised by a certain quality.[3]

Though about judgments, we can use a comparable definition for claims. In talking of persons, it appears that Joad considers only people to be subjects.

Example 5 (on the phone)
Suzy: Did Dick like the jam I made?
Zoe: Dick is right now enjoying eating your jam on toast.

Analysis Is what Zoe said subjective? According to Joad her judgment has to be about her experience for it to be subjective. So what Zoe said is objective, while if Dick says, "I'm right now enjoying eating Suzy's jam on toast" then what he's said is subjective.

According to Joad's definition whether a claim is subjective depends on who said it. Perhaps we could modify his definition so that a subjective claim is about any person's experience being modified. But it's not clear what's meant by an experience being modified, and it would classify Example 2, "The starfish is afraid of being touched," as objective.

• *Definition 4* James A. Gould says:

> Subjective: that which refers to the knower; that which exists in the consciousness but not apart from it.[4]

There are two different definitions here. The first would not apply to "Dick feels cold" if he were not reflecting on it. The second requires a definition of "consciousness" before it can be used, so it will not aid us in establishing rules for reasoning about whether there is consciousness.

• *Definition 5* Richard Foley says in his definition of "subjectivism":

> Any philosophical view that attempts to understand in a subjective manner what at first glance would seem to be a class of judgments that are objectively true or false—i.e., true or false independently of what we believe, want or hope.[5]

Foley talks as if judgments are true or false, but it's claims that are true or false. We can however, take his criterion to apply to claims: A claim is subjective if and only if it is true or false independently of what we believe, want, or hope, where we have to understand "we" to include any person at all.

Example 6 Dick: I feel cold.

Analysis According to this revised version of Foley's definition, this would be objective, since it is true independently of anything anyone believes, wants, or hopes.

Foley's definition applied to claims rather than judgments isn't going to be helpful to us since it excludes claims about sensations and a lot of other mental states. Further, to clarify what's meant by being true independently of anything anyone believes, wants, or hopes is not a trivial problem.

• *Definition 6*   A claim is subjective if and only if it is about the thought of someone or some thing.

Example 7   Zoe: Dick is hungry.

   Analysis   Zoe asserts this after watching Dick get irritable, as she remembers that he hasn't eaten for a long time and that he always gets cranky in this way when he's hungry. Dick, however, is not thinking at all about whether he's hungry. So by this definition, the example is not subjective if Dick isn't thinking about it at the time it's asserted. It might be said that he does have thoughts, just not conscious ones. But then the definition doesn't seem to do any work except point us to try to identify unconscious thoughts, as discussed in "Rationality" in this volume.

• *Definition 7*   A claim is subjective if and only if it is about the mental life of someone or some thing.

   This sounds like what we want. But there are two problems. First, it assumes that some creatures or things have a mental life. Don't get us wrong. We, the authors, do believe that other people have mental lives. If we didn't believe that about each other we wouldn't have collaborated in this investigation. If we didn't believe it about people in general, we wouldn't have bothered to write this essay. We believe further that some animals think, believe, and feel, particularly dogs.[6] But we don't want to settle that issue with a definition. We can rectify that problem by recasting the definition as:

   A claim is subjective if and only if it is *meant to be* about the mental life of someone or some thing.

Even then, this assumes that we understand and agree about what is meant by "the mental life of a creature." And that just isn't so.

   But a bigger problem remains: To use this definition we have to have a reasonably clear idea of what we mean by saying that a claim is about some topic. There has been very little research on how to reason taking into consideration the subject matter of a claim. The most extensive work on that we know is Epstein's subject matter relatedness logic; that formal system is based on the view that the subject matter of a claim is the sum of the subject matters of its parts, which severs the subject matter of a claim from the truth or falsity of the claim.[7] But other developments are surely possible.

Though this definition is what we would like to use, we also would like to avoid the problems inherent in it. So we will use it as a guide, a motive, for a definition that is based on a clearer standard.

A definition of "subjective claim"

Subjective form   A claim is in *subjective form* if it is of the form:

[Someone, or some people, or some thing(s)]
thinks/believes/feels/wants . . .

Simple subjective claims   A *simple subjective claim* is a claim that is in subjective form or is equivalent to one in subjective form.

Here two claims are ***equivalent*** means that for any way the world could be, they are both true or both false.

The bracketed part is meant to be replaced by either a name for a person or thing or a quantification over persons or things like "someone," or "almost everyone in this room," or "every dog in Bogota." The ellipses in the form can be replaced by any words that result in the sentence being a claim. The words "thinks," "believes," "feels" can be in any tense or mood, like "thought," or "would believe," or "is felt."

Example 8   Dick is cold.

Analysis   Whether this is subjective depends on whether we accept that it is equivalent to "Dick feels cold," which is clearly subjective.

This definition appears to give a linguistic standard for what counts as a subjective claim. But it relies on what equivalences we draw among claims. In some cases that will depend on the metaphysics we adopt, in others it may depend only on our understanding of certain words. As we progress, reasoning together, we can fix our agreements about such equivalences, creating a longer list of ***subjective terms*** for what counts as a subjective form. Let's begin with the following list, motivated by our idea that the terms should be about the mental life of a creature or thing.

thinks
believes
feels
wants
hopes
knows
wonders whether
is hot
is cold
is hungry
is angry
is tired
is afraid

By focusing on the linguistic standard and then on the equivalences we propose or adopt, we can arrive at some standard for classifying claims that is clear enough for many of us to use together. It will not be one that is permanently fixed but is always open to adding or deleting subjective terms. In the process of deciding what words or phrases go on our list we will have a clearer idea of our differences about what constitutes a mental life.

In the examples that follow, we'll make judgments about claims being objective or subjective according to what we consider would be common assessments. Those, as much else here, will be always open to revision.

Example 9   If Spot is a dog, then Dick is hungry or Dick is not hungry.

Analysis   We have that "Dick is hungry" is subjective. But does that mean the example is subjective?

On the classical reading of "If . . . then . . ." the claim is true no matter how the world could be. So it is equivalent to "2 + 2 = 4." So it seems it isn't subjective. But it is also equivalent to, "Dick is hungry or Dick is not hungry," which does seem to be subjective.

Using relatedness subject matter logic, the claim is not equivalent to either of these latter claims, for part of the subject matter of the claim is Dick's purported mental state of being hungry and part of it is that Spot is a dog.

So shall we classify the example as subjective or objective?

We want to avoid giving an answer that depends heavily on which logic is chosen. We'll pursue instead a substitutional analysis that will rule out this example as a subjective claim.

We start with the following definition.

A claim does not appear essentially in another claim   A claim *does not appear essentially* in another claim if all occurrences of it can be replaced by any other claim and the truth-value of the whole is unaffected.

Note that by this definition every claim appears essentially in itself.

If we say that a claim is subjective if and only if it is a simple subjective claim or has a simple subjective claim that appears essentially in it, then the last example is not subjective. But consider the following example.

Example 10   Tom was in the room when Dick said, "Zoe feels sick today."

Analysis   For evidence whether this is true or false we could, if it were available, listen to a tape recording made at that time. We don't need to know anything about the mental state of Tom or Dick, even though "Zoe feels sick today" appears essentially in it. We need to exclude claims like these from being subjective, and we can do so by requiring that a simple subjective claim that appears essentially in the claim is used, not mentioned.

But what about:

(‡)   Tom was in the room when Dick said that Zoe feels sick today.

This means not just that Dick uttered those words but that he meant to communicate roughly what those words mean. To decide whether this is true we have to judge whether Dick had an intention to communicate and also whether one phrase is equivalent in meaning to another. So the claim should be, we believe, subjective. That's not because of the phrase "Zoe feels sick today" in it but rather because of the words "said that." So let's add "said that" and other phrases that introduce indirect speech to our list of subjective terms. Some may disagree and wish to classify (‡) as objective along with other claims in which a simple subjective claim appears only in indirect speech or in an oblique context. We'll leave to them to provide examples and then modify the definition that follows

Example 11 Birds belonging to all the chief orders ruffle their feathers when angry or frightened.

Charles Darwin, *The Expression of the Emotions in Man and Animals*

Analysis "This bird is angry" and "This bird is afraid" are simple subjective claims, so it seems that this claim should be classified as subjective. But those claims don't appear in the example as stated. We have to rewrite the claim as "If a bird of any of the chief orders is angry or frightened, then it will ruffle its feathers." That rewriting is drawing an equivalence. So for compound claims we have to consider equivalences, too.

Subjective and objective claims A claim is *subjective* if and only if:

It is a simple subjective claim

or   It is equivalent to a claim in which a simple subjective claim A appears essentially, and A is not just mentioned.

A claim that is not subjective is *objective*.

This is our definition of "subjective claim." In the work that follows you can judge whether you think it is apt, starting with a series of examples.

Examples of classifying claims

Example 12 This is a fork.

Analysis It seems that this is objective: no simple subjective claim appears in it. And intuitively that seems right: There's nothing about a mental state in this claim.

But some disagree. They say that a fork is something that is of a certain size and shape that can be picked up by a person and which is designed to spear food to aid a person in eating. So to classify something as a fork can be only relative to what someone designs, which is a mental state. So the claim is subjective. But for that to yield a classification of the claim as subjective, we need that the example is equivalent to:

(*) This is something that is designed to spear food to aid a person in eating.

And we need to add "designs" to our list of subjective terms.

By using our definition of "subjective claim" we can reduce the
question of whether this claim is subjective to the question: Is the
example equivalent to (*)? We'll not try to resolve that here.

Example 13   Masreel isn't normal: she can't feel pain.

Analysis   For any subjective term T we should include "can T" in
our list of subjective terms, too, for we use the same kind of evidence
and the same kind of reasoning to evaluate, for example, "Masreel feels
pain" and "Masreel can feel pain." And we use the same kind of
evidence and the same kind of reasoning to evaluate "Masreel can't
feel pain," which is subjective since "Masreel can feel pain" appears
essentially in it.

Example 14   It's possible that Spot is hungry.

Analysis   It seems that this claim is subjective because the simple
subjective claim "Spot is hungry" appears essentially in it. But many
disagree and say that the claim is or should be understood as:

"Spot is hungry" is possibly true.

In that case "Spot is hungry" is only being mentioned, not used, so the
claim would not be subjective.

Still, it seems to us that it should be classified as subjective since
even on the last reading it's about ways that "Spot is hungry" could be
true. Let's accommodate that by simply accepting that claims of the
form "It is possible that A" and "It is necessary that A" are subjective
when A is subjective.

Example 15   You should think about dogs more often.

Analysis   Whether or how to rewrite this claim as having a simple
subjective part is not at all obvious. Whether classifying prescriptive
claims as subjective or objective even makes sense is not obvious, as
you can read in "Reasoning with Prescriptive Claims" in *Prescriptive
Reasoning*. So we'll leave prescriptive claims outside the scope of our
classifications here.

Example 16   Pythagoras discovered the theorem about right triangles
that is named after him.

Analysis   This is subjective. It doesn't matter whether you think
that mathematical theorems are abstract objects which exist independently of us or are human creations. To discover a thing is to come to
know of it, and "knows" is a subjective term.

Example 17 Tom: Ralph is a pet. Ralph barks. So I think that Ralph is a dog.

Analysis The conclusion here isn't subjective, even though it is apparently about what Tom thinks. Tom is concluding "Ralph is a dog" and the words "I think" indicate some uncertainty about whether that really follows from the premises of his argument. We often take words such as "I think" and "I believe" as comments about the conclusion of an argument, used by the person to show that he or she has some doubt about whether the conclusion is really true or really follows.[8]

Example 18 Ravi: I think I was a turtle in a former incarnation.
       Dick: Really? I thought that people who believe in reincarnation didn't believe they were any specific kind of animal but just that they were previously some kind of animal or creature.
      Ravi: No. I think I was once a turtle.

Analysis The last claim that Ravi made is subjective. He's not commenting on "I was a turtle."

Example 19 Zoe's mother: It seems to me that there's a bird on that branch.

Analysis Zoe's mother's eyesight isn't very good, and she knows she's often wrong. She needs glasses, and she is unsure about whether what appears to her to be in the distance is actually there. She really means that it seems to her that there is a bird on that branch. So her claim is subjective.

Example 20 Dick: It seems to me that the stock market is going to go down next week.

Analysis Whether this is subjective depends on whether we view "It seems to me that" as just a phrase to indicate that Dick is asserting "The stock market is going to go down next week" with less than full confidence. But if two weeks later Zoe says to him that he was wrong, he might say that he was just reporting on what seemed to him, and in that case the example would really be subjective.

Example 21 (Example 1 again) Wanda weighs more than 110 kgs.

Analysis This is an objective claim. To verify whether it is true we can ask Wanda to get on a scale and then check whether the scale registers more than 110 kgs. Though that requires our registering our perceptions, the claim is not equivalent to one about those perceptions.

Example 22   Suzy: This lemon tastes sour.

Analysis   This is a subjective claim: If "tastes" isn't already on our list, we can add it, since we think that tasting is a kind of feeling.

Example 23   This lemon is sour.

Analysis   Philosophers take this to mean that the lemon has the capability, the capacity, the power to create a sensation of sourness in the mouth of any normal person who eats it. This is often stated as: The lemon has the secondary quality of being sour.[9] The sourness is in the lemon, though the taste of sourness is in us. So the example is equivalent to:

> For any person, if that person is normal and if that person were to eat this lemon, then the lemon would taste sour to him or her.

Since we added "tastes" to our list of subjective terms, the claim is subjective.

Example 24   God exists.

Analysis   Whatever we mean by "God" it's supposed to be something that exists independently of people and any other living thing: "God exists" is not equivalent to "I believe that God exists." So the claim is objective.

But many religious traditions mean by "God" a thing that is, among other qualities, all-knowing. So to debate whether there is a God is to debate whether there is a creature that has certain mental states. Within such a tradition the example would be subjective, since "knows" is a subjective term.

Example 25   There are an even number of stars in the sky.

Analysis   This claim is objective, but no one knows how to find out whether it's true or false, and it's not likely we'll ever know.

Example 26   Zoe (to Dick): Zeke loves Zelda.

Analysis   This claim is subjective: if "loves" is not already on our list of subjective terms, let's add it. Dick and Zoe disagree about whether it's true or false, but not for lack of evidence. There's plenty; the problem is how to interpret it.

Example 27   [Example 4 again] Spot is in pain.

Analysis   Spot is whining after being bitten by a cat, he's licking his paw where it's bleeding badly, and he's limping. So we'd all agree that the example is true. Still, it's subjective, since we all take "is in pain" as a kind of feeling and hence can add that as a subjective term.

We've seen that whether a claim is objective or subjective does not depend on:

- How many people believe it.
- Whether it's true or false.
- Whether anyone can know whether it's true or whether it's false.

The subjectivist fallacy The *subjectivist fallacy* is to infer that since there's a lot of disagreement about whether a claim is true, it's subjective.

The objectivist fallacy The *objectivist fallacy* is to infer that since there's almost no disagreement about whether a claim is true, it's objective.

Intersubjective claims

A subjective claim can be true or it can be false. Some subjective claims are judged to be true by almost everyone. And some, such as "Spot is not in pain" in the circumstances of Example 27, would be judged to be false by almost everyone.

Intersubjective claims A subjective claim is *intersubjective relative to a particular group* if almost everyone in that group would agree on its truth-value. If the group is meant to be almost everyone, then the claim is simply *intersubjective*.

Example 28 Zoe: Dick really likes Suzy's chicken-peanut-butter fricassee.

Analysis Zoe and Dick are at Suzy's place for a dinner party and Suzy has served them a dreadful concoction. But Dick remembers how Zoe gets mad at him and how Suzy gets upset when he criticizes Suzy. So he pretends, and pretends very well, that he likes the awful mess he's been served. Everyone at the party believes him. So the claim is intersubjective for all those people at the party. But it's false. We can be wrong about the truth-value of an intersubjective claim.

Example 29   Zoe: That tie is ugly.

> Dick: What are you talking about? This tie looks great. It's definitely not ugly.
>
> Zoe: You're crazy, it's ugly, and if you wear it I won't go to the party with you.

Analysis   We don't have criteria for what counts as an ugly tie independent of what anyone thinks, believes, feels or wants. Indeed, we often talk of someone's "tastes" in ties or clothing. So let's add "is ugly" to our list of subjective terms. Then Zoe's first claim is subjective. So, it seems, Dick is *mistaking a subjective claim for an objective one* by arguing with Zoe: There's no contradiction between what she said and what he said.

But we often do argue like this, and the debate doesn't seem pointless, though no one is proposing a standard that isn't subjective. It's that both Dick and Zoe think that their opinion about the tie is held by most people they know, or perhaps even a wider community. Each believes that "This tie is ugly" is intersubjective, though they disagree about what truth-value almost everyone (among their friends?) would agree it has.

Example 30   [continuing the last example]

> Zoe: Almost all of our friends would think that tie is ugly.

Analysis   Zoe has made explicit her belief that the claim "This tie is ugly" is intersubjective. Of course she could be wrong: perhaps all the men would think it's great and all the women would think it's ugly.

Zoe's claim is a general subjective claim.

Particular and general subjective claims   A simple subjective claim is *particular* if it's grammatical subject refers to one person or thing. A *general* subjective claim is a quantification over many particular subjective claims.

Is every intersubjective claim A equivalent to a general subjective claim "(Almost) everyone (in this group) thinks that A"? Example 27 "Spot is in pain" is a particular subjective claim that is intersubjective, but it is not equivalent to "(Almost everyone) would judge that Spot is in pain." And "All cats can think" is a general subjective claim that is not intersubjective.

Example 31   Maria: It's cold outside.

   Analysis   We're not justified in saying that this is a claim unless we understand what Maria meant. Perhaps she means:

   I would feel cold were I outside.

In that case, it's subjective.

   Or perhaps she means:

   I and almost everyone I know would feel cold were we outside.

This is a subjective claim, too, a general one.

   Or perhaps Maria means:

   It's less than 5°C outside.

In that case the sentence is an objective claim.

Example 32   Suzy: Pablo Picasso is a better painter than Salvador Dali.

   Analysis   This is not a claim until we know what criteria Suzy has in mind. If she's using a measure such as the number of paintings each person made and the amount of money those paintings earned at auctions in the last ten years, then it's an objective claim. If she means that she prefers Picasso's work to Dali's, it's a particular subjective claim. If she has no clear idea what criteria she's using, perhaps just repeating what she heard someone say, the sentence is not a claim.

   Though art historians and critics might hope to establish objective criteria for sentences about the value of art, no such criteria have gained widespread acceptance. Perhaps all such sentences are just particular subjective claims. If they are, then there's no contradiction with what Suzy said if Tom says "Salvador Dali is a better painter than Pablo Picasso." His claim and Suzy's should be understood as meaning "better to my taste" or simply "better for me." Art critics could disagree and have no reason for disputing. Someone who holds that view is a *subjectivist in aesthetics.*

   Most art historians and critics are loath to say that all claims about value in art are particular subjective claims. They attempt to develop through dialogue, often over generations, criteria which, though subjective, (almost) all persons familiar with that area of art would agree on. Once such criteria are formulated, members of the profession then look to acceptance of those as indicative that a person is know-ledgeable in the area, thus reinforcing the intersubjective professional criteria. We can say that art critics are, or aim to be, *intersubjectivists in aesthetics.* Even then, most would hesitate to hold that we have any criteria that guarantee that claims comparing art from different cultures are intersubjective. *Value subjectivists* go further. They say that all claims about value are subjective: claims in aesthetics, ethics, politics, economics, ... *Complete subjectivists* go further still and say that all claims are subjective, abandoning the idea of any criteria of truth beyond each individual's perceptions.

Example 33   It's wrong to kill people.

Analysis   This is a value judgment. Some say that all values require the existence of beings with mental states, more specifically beings who can derive pleasure or displeasure from some states of affairs or anticipations of some states of affairs. Hence, value claims, they say, are all subjective. But at least for members of the same species the sources of pleasure and displeasure are very largely overlapping, for example, no one wants to be hungry, unsheltered, mistreated, without meaningful work, exposed to cats, ... Hence, they say, many value claims though subjective are intersubjective.

But it is not enough to talk about creatures having mental states as a prerequisite for the claim to be true to establish that the example is subjective. That's too unclear a standard. By our definitions, to show that the claim is subjective, one would have to exhibit an equivalent claim in which a simple subjective claim appears essentially. It is hardly obvious how to do that, and a general method for all value claims seems even more difficult.

Personal standards

Some claims are said to invoke personal standards or impersonal standards.

Example 34   Harry: That's an expensive car.

Analysis   When Harry said this about a new car, what did he mean? Perhaps:

The price of that car seems like a lot of money to me.
    A personal standard, and subjective.
That car costs more than I earn in a year.
    A personal standard, and objective.
The price of that car seems like a lot of money to all the students at this college.
    An interpersonal standard, and subjective.

That car costs more than any of the students at this college earn in a year.

An interpersonal standard, and objective.

That car costs more than $100,000.

An impersonal standard, and objective.

Example 35   Wanda is fat.

Analysis   Wanda is 1.62 m tall. Suppose we interpret this sentence to mean:

Wanda weighs more than 90 kg and is less than 1.65 m tall.

Then the standard uses reference to a particular person, and if we were to vary that reference to another person the truth-value of the sentence could be different. So it seems that the claim uses a personal standard.

But it seems that the claim should be classified as impersonal, since anyone would evaluate its truth-value in the same way.

It's not at all clear what in general counts as a personal standard or as an impersonal standard. However, in limited though fairly general contexts we can often be precise, as in "Reasoning with Prescriptive Claims" in *Prescriptive Reasoning* in this series. In any case, if you agree with the classifications in Example 34, a division of claims into personal, interpersonal, and impersonal does not correspond to the division of claims into particular subjective, general subjective, and objective. Nor, as in the second reading of Example 34, need a personal claim whose truth-value is agreed on by almost everyone be intersubjective.

Judgment

The definitions we first surveyed suggest that we should consider a division of claims into those which require human judgment in evaluating whether they are true and those that don't.

Example 36   Inspector: Your restaurant failed this inspection.
    Restaurant owner: That's just what you think.

Analysis   The criteria for passing a restaurant inspection include "There is an accessible sterilizing solution with test strips," "No drinks without lids are in the food preparation area," . . . , each of which is objective. But despite officials trying to write regulations that are very precise and specific, for an inspector to decide whether each of those is true depends on his or her judgment. What counts as accessible? What are the boundaries of the food preparation area? Different competent inspectors might disagree. So when the restaurant owner says, "That's just what you think," he's wrong if he means that the claim is subjective, but he might be right if he means that he disagrees with the inspector's judgment about whether certain criteria are satisfied and that other inspectors would disagree, too.

Example 37 $1 + 1 = 2$

Analysis This claim is often pointed to as one that is not only true but requires no human judgment to evaluate that it is true. Yes, it requires us to know the meaning of the "words" in it, but no more.

Yet some disagree. They take it to be like a claim in science that is not true or false except in application.[10] And the claim is clearly false when we apply it to drops of water: 1 drop of water + 1 drop of water $\neq$ 2 drops of water. To say that this is not an appropriate application of this claim is to use our judgment about what counts or doesn't count as a counterexample to it.

It is not obvious that any claim has such a precise meaning that it does not require some judgment in evaluating whether it is true or false. To say that the evaluation of whether a particular claim (or kind of claim) requires no judgment is just to say that we have an agreed-on method of evaluation that rarely leads to any disagreement, a method we don't even think about anymore. People acknowledge that the evaluation involves judgment only when they're challenged.

It seems, though, that some claims require more judgment in evaluating whether they are true or false. But to try to set out a division of claims on that basis seems hopeless, as discussed in "Truth and Reasoning" in *Prescriptive Reasoning*.

Converting subjective claims into objective ones?

Scientists prefer to deal with objective claims and often try to replace subjective claims with objective ones.

Example 38 Wanda is obese.

Analysis In the past this was a value judgment that most people took to be subjective like "That tie is ugly." But nutritionists and physicians now give objective criteria for what counts as an obese person in terms of body weight and height.

Most of us now, we suspect, would classify the example as objective, thinking of that standard, even if we can't state it exactly.

Example 39 Wanda has a compulsion to eat.

Analysis This is a subjective claim. We think that to describe someone as having a compulsion is to ascribe a kind of thinking or feeling to him or her, and would be willing to add "has a compulsion" to our list of subjective terms.

Psychologists might try to turn the example into an objective one by saying that someone has a compulsion to eat if she spends lots of money on weight-loss programs, says she needs to lose weight, says she understands that her weight can lead to diabetes and that it's making her knees and back hurt, yet continues to eat more than twice as many calories as she needs in order to maintain her current weight. In doing so they replace the subjective claim of this example with an objective claim about Wanda's behavior. But as psychologists learn more about the motives of people, they might change the behavioral criteria they use. That is, they would modify how they think this subjective claim might be correlated to but not replaced by an objective one.

Example 40 Dick: I feel cold.

Analysis This is a subjective claim.

Suppose a scientist doing research on brain waves has managed to show that Dick's neurons firing in a certain pattern is exactly correlated, time and again, with Dick saying apparently truthfully that he feels cold. The scientist then might say that the subjective "I [Dick] feel cold" can be replaced with the objective "Dick's brain waves are in this pattern," asserting that the claims are equivalent.

You might think that if scientists could do this generally for claims about people feeling cold, we could replace all subjective claims like this one with objective ones in our reasoning. But even then it is the stuff of science fiction that we would carry around with us machines that allow us to read the neuronal firing of others along with descriptions of the subjective claims they are equivalent to. Moreover, there seems to be a great difference between describing a person being in a particular neural state and describing him or her as feeling cold. We would still need to be able to state "Feeling cold is perfectly correlated with having a brain state of this type." Study of brain states can illuminate our understanding of subjective claims, but would not make the subjective/objective distinction irrelevant.

Reasoning

What counts as good reason to believe a claim? We'll set out here the basic ideas developed in the essays "Arguments" in this volume.

Plausible claims   A claim is *plausible* to a particular person at a particular time if:

- The person has good reason to believe it.
- The person recognizes that he or she has good reason to believe it.
- The person believes it.

Good reason to believe need not be through reasoning. When Dick bends over and pets Spot, he has good reason to believe "Spot is in front of me," though not through any reasoning.

Plausibility is not an either-or classification. We have an informal scale for each of the conditions, from better reason to believe to worse reason to believe, from recognizing clearly to being oblivious, from believing strongly to strongly disbelieving. Combined, we have an informal scale from the least plausible to the most plausible.

Though we do not have precise measures of plausibility, we can often compare the plausibility of claims and by being explicit about our background we can usually agree on whether we accept them as plausible. If we did not think that we can share many of our judgments of what is plausible, we would have no motive for trying to reason together. So in what follows, if we say a claim is *plausible* without specifying a particular person, we mean it's plausible to most of us now. A claim is *implausible* or *dubious* if it's not plausible.

We circumscribe to some extent what we mean by good reason to believe a claim with two principles. As a start, we define two claims to be ***contrary*** if it's not possible for them both to be true at the same time in the same way.

Good reason and contrary claims   If someone has good reason to believe a claim, then he or she does not have good reason to believe a contrary of it.

Suspending judgment   If someone does not have substantially better reason to believe a claim than to believe a contrary of it, then he or she does not have good reason to believe either of them. In that case he or she should suspend judgment on whether the claim is true.

Sometimes we use reasoning to establish a good reason to believe a claim. When we do, we are using arguments.

Arguments   An *argument* is an attempt to convince someone (possibly yourself) that a particular claim called the **conclusion** is true. The rest of the argument is a collection of claims called **premises** which are given as reasons for believing the conclusion is true.

An argument is *good* means that it gives good reason to believe the conclusion of it. To do that, the premises must be plausible. But they also must be more plausible than the conclusion, that is, the argument does not **beg the question**. Further, the conclusion has to follow from the premises.

Valid argument   An argument is *valid* if it is impossible for the premises to be true and conclusion false at the same time and in the same way.

Strong and weak arguments   An argument is *strong* if it is possible but unlikely for the premises to be true and conclusion false at the same time and in the same way; it is *weak* if it is neither valid nor strong.

The conclusion follows from the premises   The conclusion of an argument *follows from* the premises of an argument if the argument is valid or strong.

An argument is either valid or it isn't. However, whether an argument is strong or weak is a matter of degree, from the weakest argument to the strongest; there is no sharp line that divides strong arguments from weak ones. But with discussion, comparing our backgrounds, we can usually agree on whether an argument is strong. So generally "That argument is strong" like "That claim is plausible" is intersubjective. We can even link the criteria for an argument to be strong with the plausibility of claims.

An argument is not strong by default   If someone offers a description of the way the world could be in which the premises are true and conclusion false, then the burden is on the person who claims that the argument is strong to show that the possibility is unlikely by adding a premise that is plausible which shows that such a possibility is unlikely.

We now have the following necessary conditions for an argument to be good:

- The premises are plausible.
- The argument does not beg the question.
- The argument is valid or strong.

Whether these conditions are sufficient is a large topic that is explored in this and the other essays in this volume. In what follows we'll assume they are sufficient.

Unless we accept some claims as plausible without reasoning to them, we can have no good reason to believe any claim. Every argument depends on taking some claim or claims as plausible, so if we were to demand an argument for every claim, we would be faced with an infinite regress.

Reasoning to objective claims from subjective premises

Can there be a good argument all of whose premises are subjective and whose conclusion is objective?

Example 41   Dick: I see a tree in the yard. Therefore, there is a tree in the yard.

Analysis   Dick seems to be reasoning well. The premise is plausible, more plausible than the conclusion. Though the argument is not valid, it seems to be strong. Harry though, challenges Dick, saying that there is not only no tree, but nothing outside Dick's own experience, repeating what he heard in his philosophy class. Or the world is just our perceptions—there need be nothing "out there." Or the world is all mind. Or Dick could be a brain kept alive in a vat of chemicals and connected with wires stimulating it activated by some malevolent cat.

Dick hears these objections and says that they're all nonsense, completely unlikely. But an argument is not strong by default, so he should be able to come up with a claim or claims to show that they are unlikely. Yet the only claims he can muster are ones like "There is an external world," "My senses properly register what is indeed in the world much or most of the time," "The world is made up of things," none of which seems more plausible than the conclusion.

For some subjective claims the truth-value of the claim depends on a person or thing apparently registering something in the world. We do not normally require of people with whom we reason that they justify that their sensory apparatus is working properly: that they are not hallucinating, or crazy, or using the word "see" metaphorically. To do so would be an unreasonable burden in argument analysis. We make such assumptions as part of how we reason with people. Yet even beyond those, we need to assume that there is an external world, that there are things, and that in normal circumstances our perceptions give us information about them in order to arrive at the objective conclusion. It is not the subjective claims alone that yield the objective conclusion, but those combined with one or more objective claims that are part of our standard background against which we classify arguments as strong. We take those assumptions as implicit, but they are no less needed for the argument to be good.

We cannot, it seems, derive an objective conclusion from only subjective premises. We need a claim that links the subjective to the objective, but that claim will be no more plausible than the conclusion, unless we take it to be part of our metaphysics, which we believe and for which we require no argument.

Yes, we act *as if* there is an "external world" that our senses give us accurate information about most of the time. That assumption allows us to navigate in the world, to create what we believe is a coherent view of the world. But pragmatic motive to act as if does not constitute good reason to believe, neither in science (see "Models and Theories" in *Reasoning in Science and Mathematics*) nor in ordinary life (see "Explanations" in *Cause and Effect, Conditionals, Explanations*).

Reasoning to subjective claims

When do we have good reason to believe a subjective claim?

Example 42   [Example 40 again] Dick: I feel cold.

    Analysis   This is subjective.

Dick says it and knows it's true. There's no argument he can make to convince himself of this. The following is accepted by even the most thorough skeptics.[11]

Reports on feelings   When someone asserts "I feel . . ." where the blank is filled with a description of some sensation, then:

- If the person believes the claim, then he or she has good reason to believe it, and it is true.
- No good argument can be given to that person for that claim.

Continuing the analysis of the example, Zoe can have doubts about whether what Dick has said is true: perhaps Dick is fibbing, or joking, or saying this just to make Suzy feel less odd while she's complaining about feeling cold. So Zoe reasons:

> Dick says he's cold.
> Dick doesn't usually lie.
> Dick is shivering.
> Dick doesn't look like he's joking.
>   Therefore, Dick feels cold.

Zoe has no choice but to invoke objective behavioral evidence for Dick's claim because she has no direct access to Dick's sensations as Dick does. But her argument is lacking. Where's the claim that connects these plausible objective premises to the subjective conclusion? There are, after all, ways the premises could be true but the conclusion false: Dick could be an automaton; Dick could be shivering from nerves in a way that looks just like shivering from cold; Dick doesn't feel anything at the moment because he's on automatic pilot while shivering; . . . .

If Zoe were to say, "I don't think those examples of how the premises could be true and conclusion false are likely — show me they are," she'd be shifting the burden of proof. An argument isn't strong by default. If Zoe wants to show the argument is strong, she should give one or more plausible claims that show those possibilities are unlikely. To see what those might be, let's consider another example.

Example 43   Dick sees Lee accidentally hit his thumb hard with a hammer. He sees Lee cursing and grimacing and shaking his hand wildly. Dick says:

> Lee is in pain.

Analysis   Dick knows from what he sees that Lee is in pain. If Dick were to try to make a good argument for that, it would have to use objective claims about Lee's behavior as premises. But then some claim linking those objective claims to the subjective conclusion is needed. We might think that Dick could use "Almost any time someone hits his thumb with a hammer and acts in this way, he's in pain." But that's less plausible to Dick than "Lee is in pain." Indeed, for Dick or for any of us in this situation it's just obvious that Lee is in pain. It seems that Dick does not need, and cannot get a good argument for "Lee is in pain" in this situation.[12]

Example 44 Tom and Zeke are taking part in an experiment being conducted at the university by Dr. Sitz. Zeke is first hooked up to a brain-scanning machine. Then Dr. Sitz hits Zeke's thumb with a hammer very hard (they're being paid a lot to do this). Zeke screams while waving his hand rapidly, and his brain waves are registered by the machine. Afterwards Zeke looks at the scan of his brain waves. Then Tom does the experiment while Zeke looks on: Dr. Sitz hits Tom's thumb very hard with a hammer while Tom is hooked up to a machine that records his brain waves. Zeke looks at the brain scan for Tom and sees that it looks just like his did when Dr. Sitz hit him with the hammer. Then Zeke says, "Oh, now I see, Tom must be feeling as I did when I hit my thumb with the hammer. He must be in pain."

Analysis   It seems that Zeke didn't believe that Tom was in pain when he saw Tom scream and wave his hand frantically. He believed it or perhaps "really" believed it only when he saw the evidence of the similar brain waves.

We don't admire Zeke for being a good reasoner, one who doesn't take "Tom is in pain" as obviously true, a claim he has good reason to believe without any argument. We say he is lacking in empathy and imagination. He's on his way to becoming a psychopath or philosopher if he trusts the images of Tom's brain scan appearing to be the same as his rather than immediately recognizing that Tom is in pain when he sees Tom screaming just as he did when he was hit with the hammer.

Example 45 Suzy is recruited for the experiment. Dr. Sitz hits her thumb very hard with a hammer while she's hooked up to the brain-scanning machine. Tom sees her scream and wave her hand wildly. Then he looks at the brain scan for her and sees that it's very different from the ones for him and Zeke.

Analysis   Tom doesn't say, "Oh, I guess I was wrong. Suzy wasn't really in pain." If he did, he'd be as nearly incapable of empathy as Zeke. Rather, Tom concludes that it's possible for some-one to be in pain in after being hit with a hammer without having the same brain wave pattern.

"Tom is in pain", "Zeke is in pain", and "Suzy is in pain" in these situations are obviously true for almost all of us, certainly for anyone we'd be willing to meet in a dark alley. It seems, then, that from lots of examples like these we can conclude by induction "Other people have thoughts, beliefs, and feelings." But that's not right. Just as obviously true to all of us is "Other people have feelings."[13] Some say that our belief in that is built into us.[14]

These are fundamental beliefs we have about the nature of the world; they are a crucial part of our metaphysics, whether we are explicit about that or not. In order to reason at all we have to start with some claims as plausible, and those of our metaphysics are ones we take as the most plausible. We cannot justify such claims, though we can revise them as we change our views about the world. Any justification, any argument with such a claim as conclusion will have to have a premise that is not more plausible to us than that claim.

Yet it seems that some people disagree.

The arguments by analogy for other people feeling pain

Example 46   The argument by analogy of behavior for other people feeling pain[15]

Zelda: Wow! That really hurt when Dr. Sitz hit my hand with that damned hammer.

Tom: Yeah, I saw that you were in that stupid experiment, too. Your brain wave scan looked just like mine. Boy, did that hurt.

Zelda: You mean that you felt pain then, too?

Tom: Huh? Of course I did.

Zelda: But you play football and get banged up all the time, while I would be screaming in pain if someone tackled me like that.

Tom: Well, I didn't say I felt pain just like you did. But it sure did hurt.

Zelda: I really doubt it was anything like what I feel. Guys are tough, and, you know, most of us girls don't think that men have any feelings at all.

Tom: Don't be stupid. I reacted just like you did when that maniac Dr. Sitz hit my hand—and you know I'm a lousy actor. If that doesn't convince you, I don't know what will.

Analysis   Tom is making an argument to try to convince Zelda that "Tom felt pain" is true. In brief it is:

I know you can't really feel a pain I have. But we're very similar in our physical reactions in similar situations. We acted very, very similarly when we got hit with a hammer. You know that you felt pain then. So I felt pain, too.

This is an analogy: Zelda should believe Tom's conclusion based on the similarities between herself and him. But she points out differences, which boil down to saying that Tom's premises could be true yet his conclusion false because men don't feel pain, only women do.

Tom thinks that's just bizarre. But he hasn't said anything to show that possibility is unlikely, which is what he has to do if he's going to convince Zelda; the argument isn't strong by default. Yet the only claim he could muster that would show that "Only women feel pain" is not likely would be something like "Men feel pain" or "I feel pain," which are obvious to him but less plausible to Zelda than the conclusion of his argument that he felt pain in that particular situation.

The argument from analogy of similar behavior can't convince someone who doesn't already believe the conclusion.

So Tom tries another argument.

Example 47 The argument from similar construction for other people having feelings[16]

Tom: Look, it isn't just that we react the same. We're built the same: we have the same nervous system, the same kind of brains, we're made up of blood, and cells, and skin, and we bleed when we're hit with a hammer, as you know. Our nervous systems react in just the same way when we're hit with a hammer. So since you felt pain, I did, too.

Zelda: We are not built just the same. I never saw you double over from the pain of menstrual cramps.

Tom: No, we're not built in exactly the same way. But the similarities in our physical make-up are the ones that matter to having pain.

Zelda: How do you know that?

Tom: Scientists have shown an exact correlation between having those properties—you know, a nervous system, and a brain like ours, and blood—and having pain. That's one of the reasons that madman Dr. Sitz was doing his experiment.

Zelda: Oh, really. And how did Dr. Sitz know that you had pain? How did he know that I had pain? He asked us, and he watched us. He concluded we had pain from that. That's just like your argument about our having similar behavior, except that Dr. Sitz wasn't trying to convince himself, or you, or me, or anyone that you can feel pain or that I can

feel pain. He was just assuming that. How is this any
better at showing that only women feel pain isn't plausible?

Analysis It isn't any better. Zelda is right. The experiments that
scientists do to show a correlation between a certain physical make-up
and the ability to experience pain are all based on assuming that the
creatures can feel pain. They are not trying to prove that Tom or
anyone else can feel pain. They are assuming that people can feel pain
and are trying to explain why that's true. Their experiments are
designed to give evidence for a causal explanation for *why* we feel
pain, not for an argument *that* we feel pain.[17] Scientific experiments
are important for helping us learn a great deal about when and under
what circumstances people feel pain—on the assumption that they
really do feel pain.

It was hard for us to come up with an imagined dialogue in which
anyone would need to be convinced that Tom felt pain when he got his
thumb hit with a hammer. Other than the exaggerated variation on
"Men don't have feelings" which we hear in our society, the only
example we could think of is someone so abnormal that she really
can't imagine another person's interior life.

The rest of us consider "Tom is in pain" in such a situation to be
not only plausible but obviously true. So why would we feel we need
to have a proof that Tom is in pain? "I believe it, but do I have good
reason to believe it?" is OK when considering a claim about a laundry
detergent. It's a major confusion, a mistake in understanding how to
reason well, when asked about a claim of our metaphysics. Claims of
our metaphysics provide the good reason for why we believe other
claims; we can't give good reason to believe them, because there are
no other claims more plausible than them from which to argue to them.
To doubt that we have good reason to believe a claim (that expresses a
part) of our metaphysics—such as "Other people feel pain," "There are
things in the world," "Nothing can both be or not be"—is to embark on
a project to construct another metaphysics or to go down the path of the
skeptic way, not an impetus to look for a good argument.[18]

The argument by similar construction points to a program for
investigation but is not a good argument, for any attempt to show that
the possibility that Tom or anyone else is one of those many things that
doesn't feel pain is unlikely will beg the question.

Still, there is a way an analogy from similar construction could be
good, could really give us justification to believe "Tom is in pain"

without getting into Tom's head to establish directly that he can feel pain. All, or most of us, could be given a revelation by God, or the gods, or Dog who smells all that just these similarities are sufficient for a creature to feel pain. And the insight from that revelation could be more plausible to us than "Tom is in pain." Adding that insight as a premise, the argument would be good. But it would not proceed from "scientific" premises. And we could hope to convince someone else of that premise only by leading him or her to a similar revelation.

Example 48 [Example 42 again] Dick: I feel cold.

Zoe (reasoning to herself):

Dick says he's cold.
Dick doesn't usually lie.
Dick is shivering.
Dick doesn't look like he's joking.
So Dick feels cold.

Analysis We can and ordinarily do judge this and similar arguments as good. That's because when pressed we invoke a further premise, "People can feel cold or hot" or perhaps only "Dick can feel cold." Given those claims which (almost) all of us take as true without any proof, the argument is good. An argument is good or bad relative to a community of reasoners, and our community shares a metaphysics of people feeling pain, heat, cold, . . . , of other people thinking, believing, knowing, wanting, ...

Example 49 [From a pamphlet for a professional sample pack of Previcox®, a pain medication for dogs, 2007]

Dogs show pain in different ways
Most animals do not express pain the way we do. Dogs with arthritis may not show the signs of pain that most people would recognize. Dogs may express the pain of arthritis through changes in their behavior, such as:

- Lying down or resting more than usual
- Reduced desire to play or interact with owners
- Difficulty rising from a resting position
- Reluctance to walk, run or jump
- Trouble climbing stairs
- Unexplained limping
- Aggressive or defensive reactions to touch
- Uncharacteristic barking or hiding

Analysis   All of us might agree that if we saw a person with these symptoms (except barking) we'd have good reason to believe that he or she is in pain.[19] But why should that convince us that the dog is in pain?

We can talk about pain thresholds and other ways of circumscribing what we mean by "similar reactions" and "similar situations" in trying to make a good argument by analogy of behavior for dogs feeling pain. But to make a good argument we need a claim that links the objective claims about the behavior of dogs to their feeling pain. And that, as in the last example, is not going to be more plausible than the conclusion that dogs feel pain.

Example 50   Dick (to Zeke, who is kicking a puppy that's yelping):
          Stop that! Dogs have feelings.
   Zeke: Yeah, sure. And next you'll be telling me that flies do, too.

   Analysis   Zeke doesn't believe that dogs have feelings. Indeed, he thinks he's refuted that by analogy.

Dick believes "The puppy feels pain," as would most of us. We learn to believe that animals feel pain in part by being told that's so by our parents and other adults when we hit a dog, but not when we step on a bug. We don't believe that flies and worms feel pain. We say they're too different from us. But how do we draw a line? How dissimilar does a creature have to be for us to doubt it can feel pain? It wasn't so long ago that people felt it was all right to beat a donkey until it fell down bleeding; asses are beasts of burden, they used to say, without feelings or a mental life, here only to serve us. In the past people used to deny that black slaves had feelings like "we" do. The issue always is the scope of our "we": How far do we extend our empathy? What is the scope of our metaphysical assumptions about feelings?

Example 51   Ooga booga! Don't walk there. The trees and rocks will hurt you because they don't want people there. The place is taboo.

   Analysis   Not so long ago people believed that rocks and trees have feelings and thoughts. Now we say that's **anthropomorphizing**. The **intentionalist fallacy** is to base our reasoning on the assumption that things that most of us believe don't have thoughts, beliefs, or feelings do have a mental life, and in particular have intentions.[20]

Example 52 [Epstein on August 14, 2010] Today I went for a walk with my two dogs about 10 a.m. It was sunny and already hot. My large older dog Birta lagged behind, as she always does in the heat. If I don't encourage her by calling, she would return to the patio and lie down in the shade until I and my small younger dog Chocolate return.

So all three of us went down to take care of the sheep and then on into the forest. There we went to the river, and the dogs went into it, got wet, became more animated, and returned to me. Then I headed off further into the forest. The dogs often go that way with me. It was cooler in the shade of the forest. We got to a place, a gate, where I often turn back. But I didn't, and continued on past it. Both dogs came with me. Usually when I go that far with the dogs, I continue on for another two miles, as I did the last couple times the previous week with the dogs when the sun was hot. The last mile and a half of it is out of the forest. After awhile, perhaps three hundred yards beyond the gate, I realized that the dogs weren't with me. I called, and Chocolate came to me. But Birta didn't. So I called some more. I continued on the walk, calling occasionally. Still no sign of Birta. So I turned around and returned by the same route to see if she had lain down in the shade along the route. Eventually I returned home along my original path with Chocolate. At home I found Birta lying in the shade under my car. She came to the gate when I got there, entered, and went to the pond and drank, put her paws in the water. She had returned to the house a little after passing the point where the longer walk typically begins, but not by retracing the route, since the fencing and gates would have been impassable for her. Most likely from that point she returned by a direct route that parallels one I've taken with her in the past.

Analysis [Epstein] This description uses only objective claims about my dogs, and it was very hard to write. At a certain point it just becomes easier to describe what Birta was doing by using subjective claims. She realized we were going on a longer walk where she would get hotter. She felt hot and didn't want to get hotter. She knew the shorter way home from the gate, and knew that she wouldn't get so hot and could lie down in the shade at home. So she went home and waited for us near the gate under my car. Moreover, those descriptions allow me to better predict what she'll do in the future.

When it becomes easier to describe our experiences by ascribing thoughts, feelings, and beliefs to other creatures, and when those descriptions yield better predictions, we're inclined to ascribe thoughts, beliefs, and feelings to them. We act *as if* they do. But again, pragmatic motive to act as if does not constitute good reason to believe. In any case, we don't get good predictions about their behavior most of the time. We get only better predictions than we would without that assumption, certainly much better than random guessing.

We can't more easily describe our experiences with rocks and trees by ascribing mental states to them, and we can't better predict what rocks and trees "will do" by assuming they have thoughts, beliefs, and feelings. So we have no pragmatic impetus to assume that rocks and trees have thoughts, beliefs, and feelings, and some reason to think they don't.[21]

Example 53   Zoe: Zeke doesn't really love Zelda, he hates her.
   Dick: Boy are you wrong. He loves her. I asked him, and he insisted he does. And he tells her he loves her. I even told him that you think he hates her, and he just laughed and said you're completely wrong.
   Zoe: I'm sure he hates her. Look how he treated her at the party last night. And I heard he hit her when they got back home.

Analysis   Zeke insists that he loves Zelda. He believes that he loves Zelda. But by assuming that he hates her, Zoe can make better predictions and assimilate the behavioral claims she knows are true about Zeke and Zelda into a clearer story about them. In doing so, though, she's assuming that she understands the totality of Zeke's motivations and what he thinks about the world better than he does. That is very risky.[22]

In these examples and discussions we've seen that:

- For any person there are subjective claims that he or she has good reason to believe without reasoning to them.

- A subjective claim that one person has good reason to believe without reasoning to it, may require reasoning for another person to have good reason to believe it.

- We cannot reason to an objective conclusion from only subjective premises without invoking an objective claim that is part of our metaphysics.

- We cannot reason to a subjective conclusion from only

objective premises without invoking a subjective claim
that is part of our metaphysics.

- Both the argument by analogy of behavior and the argument by
  similarity of construction for other people having feelings can be
  made strong only by our assuming some claim that other people
  have feelings, which defeats the purpose of those arguments.[23]
  However, such an "argument" could be a good explanation.

We have concentrated in this section on reasoning to claims about
feelings and sensations. Reasoning about thoughts and beliefs is more
difficult because of the large disagreements about the nature of those.

Conclusion

We can get good arguments from subjective to objective but only
relative to our metaphysics, relative to our usually implicit assumption
that there is a world external to us and that our senses usually give us
accurate information about it.

We can get good arguments from objective to subjective but only
relative to our metaphysics, relative to our usually implicit assumption
that other people have thoughts, beliefs, and feelings.

There is a gap between our objective beliefs and our subjective
beliefs that cannot be bridged by reasoning. There is a gap between
our subjective beliefs about ourselves and our subjective beliefs about
others. That does not mean that we cannot have good reason that
bridges the gap. But such good reason will be part of our metaphysics,
or part of our culture, or part of our biological nature, or part of what
God or Dog or the gods have determined we should believe.

Bertrand Russell in "Mysticism and Logic" said:

> Of the reality or unreality of the mystic's world I know nothing.
> I have no wish to deny it, nor even to declare that the insight which
> reveals it is not a genuine insight. What I do wish to maintain—and
> it is here that the scientific attitude becomes imperative—is that
> insight, untested and unsupported, is an insufficient guarantee of
> truth, in spite of the fact that much of the most important truth is
> first suggested by its means. p. 12 (I.1)

But all our metaphysics can be justified at best by such insights.
Between us and the world, and between us and each other, there is a
gap, a gap that can be filled only with insight, imagination, empathy,
revelation, faith, . . . , but not by reasoning.

NOTES

1. (p. 95) For example, Thomas Nagel's paper "What Is It Like to Be A Bat?" has interesting ideas related to our work here, but it is difficult to evaluate them because of his unclear notion of subjective and objective. He speaks of "the subjective character of experience" (p. 436), "subjective phenomenon" (p. 437), "phenomenological facts are perfectly objective" (p. 442), "the objective nature of the things" (p. 443), and he takes the divide to be a continuum when he says "The less it depends on a specifically human viewpoint, the more objective is our description" (p. 444).

Subjectivity, as opposed to how to reason with subjective claims, has a long history in Western philosophy; see Ronald de Sousa, "Twelve Varieties of Subjectivity: Dividing in Hopes of Conquest."

2. (p. 96) Compare Karl R. Popper in *The Logic of Scientific Discovery*:

> My use of the terms 'objective' and 'subjective' is not unlike Kant's. He uses the word 'objective' to indicate that scientific knowledge should be *justifiable*, independently of anybody's whim; a justification is 'objective' if in principle it can be tested and understood by anybody. p. 44

Kai Nielsen in "Ethics, Problems of" says:

> A moral judgment is objective if, and only if, it is either true or false and if its truth does not depend on the peculiarities of the person who makes the judgment or on the culture to which he belongs, but shall be determinable by any rational agent who is apprised of the relevant facts. p. 126, Volume 3

3. (p. 97) *Guide to Philosophy*, p. 331.

4. (p. 98) *Classical Philosophical Questions*, p. 664.

5. (p. 98) "Subjectivism," p. 773.

6. (p. 99) We disagree about cats.

7. (p. 100) See *Propositional Logics* by Epstein and "Relatedness predicate logic" by Epstein and Stanislaw Krajewski.

8. (p. 105) See the analysis of indicator words in "Arguments" in this volume.

9. (p. 106) See, for example, James Rachels, "Naturalism", p. 86.

10. (p. 112) See "Mathematics as the Art of Abstraction" in *Reasoning in Science and Mathematics*.

11. (p. 117) See Benson Mates, *The Skeptic Way: Sextus Empiricus' Outlines of Pyrrhonism*.

12. (p. 118) Perhaps this is the view of Ludwig Wittgenstein:

> "I can only *believe* that someone else is in pain, but I *know* it if I am." — Yes: one can make the decision to say "I believe he is in pain" instead of "He is in pain". But that is all.—What looks like an explanation here, or like a statement about a mental process, is in truth an exchange of one expression for another which, while we are doing philosophy, seems the more appropriate one.
>
> Just try—in a real case—to doubt someone else's fear or pain.
> *Philosophical Investigations*, section 303

Compare also Alvin Plantinga in "Is Belief in God Properly Basic?"

> If I see someone displaying typical pain behavior, I take it that he or she is in pain. Again, I don't take the displayed behavior as *evidence* for that belief; I don't infer that belief from others I hold; I don't accept it on the basis of other beliefs. Still, my perceiving the pain behavior plays a unique role in the formation and justification of that belief; as in the previous case, it forms the ground of my justification for the belief in question. p. 45

13. (p. 120) Compare "There are things in the world" as discussed in "Base Claims," pp. 82–83 in this volume.

14. (p. 120) See the discussion in *Baboon Metaphysics: The Evolution of a Social Mind* by Dorothy L. Cheney and Robert M. Seyfarth.

15. (p. 120) The argument from analogy of behavior for not just pain but feelings or thoughts has been made so many times that we don't associate it with anyone in particular. It goes back at least to David Hume (*A Treatise of Human Nature*, bk. I, pt. 3, sect 16), and Bertrand Russell used it in *Human Knowledge, Its Scope and Limits*. Alec Hyslop refers to it as the "traditional" argument for other minds in his article "Other Minds" and reviews the standard difficulties that people raise for it. We've not tried to put it in its most general form here because the problems with it are much clearer in a particular example, which you can generalize if you wish.

16. (p. 121) For a fuller discussion of the argument from similar construction, see William S. Robinson, "Some Nonhuman Animals Can Have Pains in a Morally Relevant Sense."

17. (p. 122) For an explanation to be good, the conclusion of it must be more plausible than its premises, because we assume the conclusion is true and are trying to show why it is. For an argument, the conclusion must be less plausible than the premises because we are trying to show that the conclusion is true. Some people think that we can use explanations as arguments through inference to the best explanation, but that is a fallacy, as shown in "Explanations" in *Cause and Effect, Conditionals, and Explanations*.

18. (p. 122) See *The Skeptic Way: Sextus Empiricus' Outlines of Pyrrhonism* by Benson Mates.

19. (p. 124) For Epstein we would expect barking.

20. (p. 124) It is easy to forget this. Nearly every day Epstein has occasion to invoke the mantra "Inanimate objects do not intend to harm you."

21. (p. 126) Some say that there isn't anything more to having thoughts and beliefs than being disposed to act in ways that make sense in light of the sentences that express what is said to be thought or believed. For those, like Daniel Dennett in *The Intentional Stance*, Example 53 would be sufficient evidence that Epstein's dog Birta thinks.

22. (p. 126) See the discussion in "Rationality" in this volume.

23. (p. 127) In a 1997 article, "Some Nonhuman Animals Can Have Pain in a Morally Relevant Sense," William S. Robinson develops a strengthened version of the argument from similar construction that he regards as good. In the other works of his cited in the bibliography here, he offers an account of attributing beliefs and wants to people, and explains how that account can be extended to beliefs and wants of non-human animals.

Generalizing

To generalize is to make an argument from premises about a part to a conclusion about the whole. How do we evaluate such arguments?

After defining what we mean by a generalization, we'll look at the standard method for evaluating generalizations, which we'll refine through a series of examples. Then we'll turn to the question of whether a generalization can be a good argument.

What is a generalization?

Claims, and arguments, and the evaluation of arguments generally are discussed in "Arguments" in this volume. Here we are concerned with generalizations, which are a specific kind of argument.

Generalizations A *generalization* is an argument in which we conclude a claim about a group or mass, called the ***population***, from a claim or claims about some part of it but not the whole, called the ***sample***. Sometimes the conclusion of the argument is called the ***generalization***; sometimes that word is used for the whole argument. The claims about the sample are called the ***inductive evidence*** for the conclusion.

Example 1   Dick: Every New Yorker any of my friends or I know is rude and pushy. So all New Yorkers are rude and pushy.

   Analysis   This is a generalization. The sample is all the New Yorkers Dick and his friends have met. The population is all New Yorkers.

Example 2   Maria: All but one of the dogs I've ever seen bark. So almost all dogs bark.

   Analysis   This is a generalization. The sample is all the dogs Maria has seen. The population is all dogs. The conclusion of a generalization need not be a universal claim.

Example 3   Of potential customers surveyed, 72% said they liked "very much" the new green color that Yoda plans to use for its cars. So about 72% of all potential customers will like it.

   Analysis   The sample is the group of potential customers interviewed, and the population is all potential customers.

   Sometimes the generalization we want and we're entitled to isn't "all," but "most," or "72%": the same proportion of the whole as in the sample will have the property. This is a statistical generalization.

Example 4   The sample of blood the doctor drew from you after you were fasting has normal glucose levels. Therefore, you have normal glucose levels in your system.

   Analysis   The sample is the blood the doctor took. It's a very small sample compared to the amount of blood you have in your body, but the doctor is confident that it is like the rest of your blood, which is the population. A generalization need not be about things; the population can be a mass and the sample a part of that.

Example 5   I should build my house with the bedroom facing this direction to catch the morning sun.

   Analysis   We believe we know where the sun will rise in the future based on where we've seen it rise in the past. The sample is all the times in the past when the sun rose: we know that the point where the sun rises varies slightly from season to season, but is roughly east. The population is all times the sun has risen or will rise, which we think will be in roughly the same direction.

Example 6   Maria goes to the city council meeting with a petition signed by all the people who live on her block requesting that a street light be put in. Addressing the city council, she says, "Everyone on this block wants a street light here."

Analysis   Maria is not generalizing. There's no argument from some to more, since the sample equals the population.

Example 7   In a study of 816 people who owned sport utility vehicles in Cincinnati, Rigochi owners expressed the lowest satisfaction with their SUVs. So Rigochi owners are less satisfied with their cars than other SUV owners.

Analysis   Here we know about the 816 people who were surveyed in Cincinnati—they are the sample. The conclusion is about all SUV owners everywhere, and they constitute the population.

Is the generalization good? That is, is the argument good? Is there any reason that we should think that these 816 people are like all SUV owners everywhere?

Evaluating a generalization

Though a mathematical theory is often invoked to judge the evidence for a generalization, the details of the mathematics are inessential to the basic ideas of the standard approach, which I'll set out here.

What can go wrong

Tom's sociology professor has assigned him to conduct a survey to find out the attitudes of students on his campus about sex before marriage. "That's easy," Tom thinks, "I'll just ask some of my friends."

So he asks all his friends he can reach on Tuesday whether they think sex before marriage is a great idea or not. Twenty of the twenty-eight say "Yes," while eight say "No."

Tom takes the results to his professor, and she asks why he thinks his friends are typical. "I guess they are," Tom responds. But, she asks, aren't they mostly your age? And the same sex as you? How many are gay? How many are married? And is twenty-eight really enough to generalize from? And what about that question? Is sex before marriage a *great* idea or not? Isn't that biased?

So Tom brainstorms with some of his friends and figures he'll ask 100 students as they leave the student union one question, "Do you approve of sexual intercourse before marriage?"

He goes to the student union at 4 p.m. on Wednesday, asks the students, and finds that 83 said "No," while 17 said "Yes." That's different from what he expected, but there was no bias in the question, and surely those 100 students are typical.

Tom presents the results to his professor, and she suggests that he should find out what was going on at the student union that day. It seems the campus Bible society was having a big meeting there that let out at 4 p.m. Maybe this survey won't give a good generalization.

So Tom and three friends get together, and at 9 a.m., 1 p.m., and 6 p.m. on Wednesday they station themselves outside the student union, the administration offices, and the big classroom building. Each is to ask the first 20 people that come by just two questions: "Are you a student here?" and "Do you approve of sex before marriage?" They get 171 people saying they are students, with 133 saying "Yes" to the second question and 38 saying "No." That's a lot of responses with no evident bias in the sampling. Tom tells his professor what they've done, and she asks, "Why do you think your sample is representative? Why do you think it's big enough?"

Representative samples

In order to be justified in concluding a claim about the population based on claims about the samples, we need good reason to think the sample is like the whole. In his last attempt to determine students' attitudes, Tom chose his sample haphazardly.

Haphazardly chosen sample A sample is chosen *haphazardly* if there was no conscious bias in selecting what is in the sample.

Does choosing a sample haphazardly give us any reason to believe it is like the whole population? No. There could be lots of ways the sample is atypical. In Tom's case, students who go to classes on Monday, Wednesdays, and Fridays might be different from those who are on campus Tuesdays and Thursdays. Or all the athletes could have been out of town for games that day. It's not that we have reason to believe the sample isn't like the whole. We just don't have reason to believe it is. What we need for a good generalization is a representative sample.

Representative sample A sample is *representative* if no part of the population appears in the sample more than its proportion in the population.

With a representative sample, we have reason to believe that what we learn about the sample will be true of the population, too.

But no sample can be representative. Any single thing in the population can be distinguished from all others and hence is a subgroup. We can only try to get a sample that is representative with respect to the aspects of things in the sample that matter. For instance, in trying to decide if a majority of people in a small town think the police are doing a good job, we don't want to have too many people in the sample who have been arrested, nor too many who never had any exposure to the police, nor . . . . But what subgroups don't matter? Those people who are blonde? Perhaps the police treat blondes differently. Those people who are short? Perhaps the police treat short folks differently. We already need to generalize in order to distinguish which subgroups of the population are "relevant" to the generalization.

We rely, therefore, on samples that are chosen in such a way that there's no greater likelihood of one subgroup being over-represented in the population than another.

Random sampling   A sample is *chosen randomly* if each time a choice is made of an object or some quantity from the population to be in the sample, there is an equal chance that any of the other objects or quantities of the population not yet chosen will be selected.

Though our definition covers sampling of masses, in what follows I'll talk only about objects, leaving to you to modify the discussions to apply to masses.

If a sample is chosen randomly and is big enough, then there is good reason to believe it will be close to representative. If a certain kind of object for which the conclusion might not hold is 14% of the population, then for each choice there is a 14% chance that one of those objects will be chosen.[1] Since the choices are independent, the chance of all objects in the sample being from that small subgroup will be very small. And the chance of no object from that subgroup being in the population is extraordinarily small. Indeed, the likelihood is that very close to 14% of the sample will be from that sample.

The law of large numbers   If the probability of something occurring is X%, then over the long run the number of occurrences will tend toward X%.

But what makes us believe this?

Suppose you have a coin. You look at it and say there's a 50% chance it will come up heads if you flip it. You bet a quarter with someone that it will come up heads and you win. You bet again, and you win again. You do that 300 times and you win 300 times. So, being no dummy, you raise your bet to $1,000 that it will come up heads.

That seems like a good bet, even though, by your first analysis, there's still just a 50% chance of winning. And according to the law of large numbers, in the long run you will lose as often as you win.

But if it came up heads 300 times in a row, you've got good reason to believe the coin isn't fair, that is, there is not an even chance that it will come up heads. How many flips of the coin begin to approximate "the long run"? Against any belief in the law of large numbers is your belief that if something is always one way in the past, it will be so in the future.

Moreover, even accepting the law of large numbers, choosing a sample randomly won't guarantee that the sample is representative. After all, it's the "long run" that will give us a representative sample. In the short run, anything might happen, even a run of 300 heads, or a sample composed entirely of convicted felons. But the likelihood of that is very small. At best what we have by choosing a sample randomly is that there is much less chance that the sample will be unrepresentative.

Sample is chosen haphazardly.
Therefore, the sample is representative.

> There are lots of ways the sample could turn out to be bad.
> This is a weak argument.
> We have little reason to believe the conclusion.

Sample is chosen randomly.
Therefore, the sample is representative.

> There are few ways the sample could turn out to be bad.
> This is a strong argument.
> We have good reason to believe the conclusion.

How do we choose a sample randomly? Mathematicians have methods for generating lists of numbers which are as random as we need (whether they are "truly" random is a question mathematicians debate). If the items in the population can be identified individually, then they can be numbered, and the sample chosen according to the numbers that appear on the list of randomly generated numbers. For example, if the population is all people who work for the city government, we can use their social security numbers.

Of course, this won't always do. The population might be all people who work in the United States. The best way of identifying them is via their Social Security numbers, and we can choose a sample that way. But that would miss all those people who work illegally without Social Security numbers. So we have to try to include some of them in the sample. How many? We have to estimate how many there are in the U.S. and try to pick some of them randomly. We will get a sample that is as close to representative as time, money, and circumstances allow.

The size of the sample

How big the sample has to be depends on how much *variation* there is in the population. If there is very little variation, and we know that, then a small sample can be representative, and there may be no need for it to be chosen randomly. Lots of variation or no knowledge about how much variation there is demands a large sample that is chosen randomly if we are to believe that the sample is representative.

How the sample is studied

Choosing a large enough representative sample is important for a generalization to be good, but it's not enough. The sample has to be studied well.

The doctor taking your blood to see if you have diabetes won't get a reliable result if her test tube is contaminated or if she forgets to tell you to fast the night before. You won't find out the attitudes of students about sex before marriage if you ask a biased question. Picking a random sample of bolts won't help you determine if they're O.K. if all you do is inspect them visually, not with a microscope or a stress test.

Necessary conditions for a generalization to be good

We've seen that a good generalization requires the following premises, whether stated or not.

Premises needed for a good generalization
- The sample is representative.
- The sample is big enough.
- The sample is studied well.

For an argument that is very precise, with mathematically quantified population, sample, and method of studying the sample, there is a well-established theory of statistics to make these claims precise. But in our daily lives our ordinary estimates of them suffice.

It's not clear whether these premises or any collection of premises are enough to establish that a generalization is a good argument. Before surveying some views about that, let's look at some examples.

Examples

Example 8   A "Grassroots Survey of Democratic Leaders" in 2005 from the Democratic National Committee asked 14 questions. Among them was:

Do you support new tax cuts targeted at working families?
—Yes, with our economy struggling, working families need a tax break.
—No, additional tax cuts at this time will only worsen the federal deficit.

Analysis   Even if we have reason to believe the sample is more or less representative, the sample wasn't studied well. There's no reason to believe any generalization from a survey that uses such biased questions.

Example 9   More than four million people younger than 21 drove under the influence of drugs or alcohol last year, according to a government report released Wednesday. That's one in five of all Americans aged 16 to 20.

Associated Press, 12/30/2004

Analysis   We don't know whether they used an anonymous questionnaire, so we don't have reason to believe that the sample was studied well, and hence we don't have good reason to accept the generalization.

Example 10   37% of the people in your town who were surveyed wear glasses, so 37% of all people in your town wear glasses.

Analysis   It's never reasonable to believe exact statistical generalizations. No matter how many people in your town are surveyed, short of virtually all of them, you can't be confident that exactly 37% of all of them wear glasses. Rather, "37%, more or less, wear glasses" would be the right conclusion.

That "more or less" can be made fairly precise according to a theory of statistics. The *margin of error* tells us the range within which the actual number for the population is likely to fall. How likely is it that they're right? The *confidence level* measures that.

Example 11 The opinion poll says that when voters were asked their preference, the incumbent was favored by 53% and the challenger by 47%, with a margin of error of 2%, and a confidence level of 95%. So the incumbent will win tomorrow.

Analysis The surveyors are concluding that the percentage of all voters who favor the incumbent is between 51% and 55%, while the challenger is favored by between 45% and 49%. The confidence level is 95%. That means there's a 95% chance it's true that the actual percentage of voters who prefer the incumbent is between 51% and 55%. If the confidence level were 60%, then the survey wouldn't be very reliable: There would be a 4-out-of-10 chance that the conclusion is false, given those premises. To summarize:

Margin of error ± 2% gives the range around 53% in which it is likely that the population value lies. It is part of the conclusion: Between 51% and 55% of all voters favor the incumbent.

Confidence level of 95% says how likely it is that the value for the population lies in that range.

The confidence level *measures the strength of the generalization as an argument.* Typically, if the confidence level is below 95%, the results won't even be announced. The bigger the sample, the higher the confidence level and the lower the margin of error. The problem is to decide how much it's worth in extra time and expense to increase the sample size in order to get a better argument.

Example 12 Dick: I went hiking today in the rain, and the water got into my boots and my feet got soaking wet. So the next time I go hiking in these boots when it's raining as hard as today my feet will get wet.

Analysis Though the sample is only one time, we have reason to believe it's representative: We can't imagine anything different in other occasions when it's raining this hard that would affect whether Dick's feet get wet when he's wearing those boots. But that means we could frame this as a valid argument:

(‡) If boots leak water hiking in one rainfall, then they are not water-proof and will always leak water in rainfall that is as heavy.
These boots leaked water hiking in a rainfall.
Therefore, these boots are not waterproof and will always leak water in rainfall that is as heavy as that one.

This is a good argument if the premises are plausible. But to say that the first premise is plausible is just to say that a sample of one is representative.

But isn't the first claim in (‡) just the generalization we wish to establish in the example? That's not obvious, since it assumes much about how we should rewrite one claim into another. In any case, we could make it more precise in terms of the nature of water and leather. *If we have good reason to believe that a sample of one or very few is representative, we can usually convert the generalization into a valid argument.*

Example 13   I [Charles Sanders Peirce] take from a biographical dictionary the first five names of poets, with their ages at death. They are,

Aagard,	died at 48	Abunowas,	died at 48
Abeille,	died at 76	Accords,	died at 45
Abulola,	died at 84		

These five ages have the following characters in common: 1. The differences of the two digits composing the number, divided by three, leaves a remainder of *one*. 2. The first digit raised to the power indicated by the second, and then divided by three, leaves a remainder of *one*. 3. The sum of the prime factors of each age, including *one* as a prime factor, is divisible by *three*.
Therefore, these characteristics are shared by the dates of death of all poets.[2]

Analysis   There's no reason to believe the conclusion based on these premises. Given any collection of objects we can find some characteristic common to them all. The fewer the items, the more characteristics we're likely to spot.

In the discussion of this example, Peirce goes into the question of hypotheses and confirmation. He says that we must start with the characteristics first, and then see if examples confirm it. He conflates the issue of how to evaluate an argument with how to evaluate an explanation, which is very different.[3]

More simply, what reason do we have to believe that the sample is representative and big enough? None whatever.

Example 14   A little more than half of all human births are male. Hence, probably a little more than half of all births in New York during any one year are male.[4]

Analysis   The conclusion is statistical, "A little more than half of all births in New York during any one year are male." The word "probably" indicates the speaker's view that the conclusion is not certain.

This is not a generalization, since it goes from more to fewer. Nor is it valid. To judge this example we have to ask whether there is any reason to believe that the births in New York might differ from all births. We have to decide whether the births in New York are (more or less) representative of all births. To the extent we are justified in believing that, we are justified in believing the conclusion. Compare:

A little more than half of all human births are male. Hence, probably a little more than half of all births in China during any one year are male.

Perhaps the births in China are not representative of all births, since there is a great prejudice there in favor of male children, and screening of fetuses may be widespread enough now that many female fetuses are aborted.

Going from more to fewer is similar to going from some to more in that we can use the words "population" and "sample" in the obvious ways, and if the premise is not universal, the sample should be representative for the argument to be good.

But how can the sample be representative if it is just one object? The difficulty again is what is meant by "representative." We substitute that we have no reason to believe that it is not just as likely that the object is drawn from any one subgroup of the population as any other.

Example 15   Any time I have been in an enclosed space with a cat for more than about fifteen minutes my eyes start itching, I start sneezing, and I get an asthma attack. Therefore, any time in the future that I end up in an enclosed space with a cat for more than about fifteen minutes my eyes will start itching, I will start sneezing, and I'll get an asthma attack.

Analysis   The sample for this generalization is, from my memory, very large (at least twenty-five times). Should I believe the conclusion?

The sample is large, studied well, and, though haphazardly chosen, should be representative enough of contact with cats. So I should not believe the conclusion is false. It's not irrational to suspend judgment. Most people would say that the argument gives good enough reason to accept the conclusion.

But what if the sample were just two times? Just twice I'd had an apparent allergy attack from a cat. And suppose I'm invited to a friend's home who has a cat. Should I believe the conclusion and decline the invitation?

The sample isn't very large, nor, perhaps, representative. And I've no reason to believe the conclusion is false. Perhaps I should suspend judgment. But given the risk of a very unpleasant evening, I act as if the conclusion were true. That needn't mean that I *believe* the claim is true. But in this case, with this evidence and risk, I act as if I did.

For choices of action, the degree of risk may determine how strong we require an argument to be before we accept the conclusion. Risk may determine our choice of action, but risk does not affect the evaluation of the argument.

Example 16   No dog I've ever seen has liked cats. So no dog likes cats.

Analysis   I made this argument, and I believe the premise. My memory might be wrong, but it's the best source of evidence about the past that I have, corrected as it might be by others' evidence.

Am I justified in believing the conclusion? Let's look at the three premises necessary for a good generalization.

Is the sample big enough? I'm not sure, but I've seen a lots of cats and dogs near each other.

Is the sample studied well? I'm not sure, since I didn't really examine the home life of the dogs and cats, but just looked at how they reacted to each other when they met. Maybe a dog would dislike all cats except those it lived with.

Is the sample representative? Is there anything special about the dogs and cats I've met? I'm not sure. How could I tell?

I've no good reason to believe that the three premises necessary for a good generalization are true. So I've no reason to think that the argument is good. I suspend judgment about the conclusion.

Example 17 Every time I look into my refrigerator, the light is on. Therefore, the light in my refrigerator is always on.

 Analysis The sample is the times I've looked into my refrigerator. Why is that representative of all times, including when I do not look into the refrigerator?

 The sample isn't representative: it was pointed out to me that I can push a small lever that the door hits when it closes and see the light go out. But even if there weren't anything obvious to push, say the light goes out when a vacuum seal is made a few minutes after the door closes, I could look at the wiring diagram for the refrigerator. I could determine whether the sample is representative.

Example 18 Any time anyone has ever been near a tree falling in the forest, the fall made noise. Therefore, any time a tree falls in a forest, it makes noise.

 Analysis If by "noise" we mean "perceived as a great sound," the argument is clearly bad. So let's take "noise" to mean "makes waves in the air that a person would perceive as noise if he or she were around."

 As for the previous example, what reason do we have to believe the sample is representative? We find lots of fallen trees where no one was around, but why should we think that noise was made when they fell?

 There's no wiring diagram we can consult. Simply invoking the regularity of nature seems no better than invoking the regularity of refrigerators.

 Rather, we have a theory of how "nature" works. Part of that theory is the assumption that the world obeys the same physical laws regardless of whether there are people around to observe. That's a metaphysical assumption, not a claim that can be proved from experience. In that theory, noise is made by falling trees regardless of whether there is a human nearby. This is our conjectured "wiring diagram" for how the world works. It's our best guess, and to the extent we believe it's true, we should believe the conclusion of this argument.

Can a generalization be a good argument?

As the examples show, we use and rely on generalizations in our lives. We also have tools to say when a generalization is bad. But can any generalization be good?[5] Let's look at some answers.

The uniformity of nature

Roughly, the principle that guarantees that generalizations are good is said to be:

> *Uniformity of nature*
> Whatever has happened in the past is likely to happen in the future in similar circumstances.

But assuming that this sentence is not so vague as to be meaningless, it's a very bad bet, as anyone who has dated more than one person or trained more than one dog can tell you. Unless, that is, you want to make "similar circumstances" precise by eliminating all anomalies. But that would be circular, since it is supposed to be similar circumstances that are guaranteeing that there are no anomalies. In any case, the evidence for this principle is less compelling than the evidence for the conclusion of most generalizations, so adding it would beg the question.

Here is what John Stuart Mill in *A System of Logic,* III. III.1 (p. 223) says in adopting such a principle:

> There is a principle implied in the very statement of what Induction is; an assumption with regard to the course of nature and the order of the universe; namely, that there are such things in nature as parallel cases; that what happens once, will, under a sufficient degree of similarity of circumstances, happen again, and not only again, but as often as the same circumstances recur. This, I say, is an assumption, involved in every case of induction. And, if we consult the actual course of nature, we find that the assumption is warranted. The universe, so far as known to us, is so constituted, that whatever is true in any one case, is true in all cases of a certain description; the only difficulty is, to find what description.

Mill says that this axiom can be the basis for converting every induction (generalization) to a valid argument. The only problem, as he notes, is what warrant we have for believing this axiom, for, as he says (p. 225), "I regard it as itself a generalization from experience." He later says that in any particular application of the principle we can be fallible, but that we shall be less fallible if we attend to noting when there are exceptions and correcting our generalizations accordingly:

> To test a generalization, by showing that it either follows from, or conflicts with, some stronger induction, some generalization based on

a broader foundation of experience, is the beginning and the end of
the logic of induction. (III.XXI.2, p. 402)

Others try to refine the principle into a sentence that is not vague
and claim it is a "transcendental" truth that we are privileged to intuit,
or that we are built to "know" or "believe"; or a good God would not
deceive us, so that it is indeed true. Otherwise, they say, it would be
just as likely for figs to appear on thistles as for apples on an apple tree.
Life would be unlivable. Sometimes it is said (though this seems to be
a generalization) that if something like the uniformity of nature weren't
true, we couldn't survive. Evolution would not work. No one could
ever predict anything, while we must be able to predict in order to
survive. But that's just to say you'll accept this principle as part of
your metaphysics, at least until shown wrong.

The problem, though, of what description is correct for a generalization is substantial, as the next two examples show.

Example 19 Every emerald anyone has ever seen is green. Therefore,
all emeralds are green.

Analysis The conclusion goes beyond the premise both in speaking of emeralds now and in the past that have not been seen, but also in
speaking of all future emeralds—assuming that our understanding of
"emerald" does not include that an emerald must be green.

Our sample is very large, though it may be haphazard in respect to
all existing emeralds. Is it representative? That question doesn't even
make sense. What does it mean for a sample of only past and existing
objects to be representative of all objects that may ever come into
existence?

Some say that not only does "representative" make sense here, but
that we have good reason to believe that the sample is representative,
invoking a principle of the uniformity of nature. But the evidence for
such a principle is less compelling than the evidence for the conclusion
of this example, so adding it would beg the question.

We have no evidence whatsoever for the contradictory of the
conclusion: "Some emeralds are not green." Therefore, we may
suspend judgment or we may accept the conclusion, depending on
how skeptical we are.

Example 20 Every emerald anyone has ever seen is green. Therefore,
all emeralds are green until the year 2099 and thereafter blue.

Analysis This argument is clearly not good. The premise gives us no reason to believe the conclusion, for the conclusion immediately entails the contradictory of the conclusion of the last example, which we said we had no reason to believe.

This example, however, can be made to seem more puzzling by defining a predicate "grue" as "green until the year 2099 and blue thereafter." Then we'd have:

(*) Every emerald anyone has ever seen is grue.
     Therefore, all emeralds are grue.

The premise of (*), it is said, is just as plausible as the evidence for the last example. So the argument should be just as good. Example 19 and this argument are symmetrical: If we accept this one as good, then we should say that Example 19 is bad.

The problem here is that we don't have any assurance that we have divided the world in the right way.[6] There will always be lots of descriptions of the world, and what Nelson Goodman has shown with this example is that any stuff (in this case emeralds that we've encountered) can be used to generalize to contradictory claims.[7]

Here is how Goodman resolves the apparent paradox (he calls claims like the conclusions of these arguments "hypotheses" or "projections").

> Suppose, for example, that we are now at the time in question in the example . . . when all emeralds examined have been green; and suppose that the hypothesis that all emeralds are grue is projected. . . . If the hypothesis that all emeralds are green is also projected, then the two projections disagree for unexamined emeralds. In saying these two projections thus conflict, we are indeed assuming that there is some unexamined emerald to which only one of the two consequent-predicates applies; . . . Yet how are we to devise a rule that will make the proper choice between these conflicting projections? We have noted that "green" and "grue" seem to be quite symmetrically related to each other.
>
> . . . The answer, I think, is that we must consult the record of past projections of the two predicates. Plainly "green", as a veteran of earlier and many more projections than "grue", has the more impressive biography. The predicate "green", we may say, is much better *entrenched* than the predicate "grue".
>
> We are able to draw this distinction only because we start from the record of past actual projections. We could not draw it starting

merely from hypotheses and the evidence for them. For every time
that "green" either was actually projected or—so to speak—could
have been projected, "grue" also might have been projected.

But the only time I can remember ever using "green" in a generalization is with just this example. Perhaps I have used it before, but I don't
recall. Perhaps lots of others have used it before, but I don't know of
those. Nonetheless, I still reject (*), and I suspect you would too, even
if you've never used "green" in a generalization before. We divide up
the world in various ways in which we have confidence. Why we have
confidence in those ways is a big question that I won't try to answer. It
may depend on our experience, or our metaphysics, or . . . . But once
we've plunked for some ways of dividing up our experience, we'll
generalize according to them, and reject generalizations that contradict
those ways. In this case, it isn't just that (*) contradicts Example 19, as
that (*) would have the very implausible consequence "Someday in the
future there will be an emerald that looks to our eyes completely different than any we've ever seen." But "looks completely different" is
probably dependent on how we divide up the world and is not so
language independent as it may seem.

This is part of the problem of how "knowledge" enters into our
evaluation of whether an argument is strong, discussed in "Arguments"
in this volume. We think we know a lot about the world, based on how
we divide it up. We're not about to reject that "knowledge" without a
good argument (based on experience?) to the contrary. But what we
take to be a good argument is going to be determined in part by the
categories we are using to divide up the world.

That isn't circular. It's rather a reflection that the categories we
use to divide up the world are entrenched in the sense that the laws of
formal logic are entrenched: We resist rejecting them in the face of
counterexamples, claiming that the counterexamples aren't "really"
counterexamples, until the number of counterexamples and the
naturalness of them finally convinces us otherwise. Entrenchment
doesn't have to do with previous generalizations, but with previous
use in our ordinary language in our ordinary life.

This is not an appeal to pragmatism, for again, the reasons we
accept certain ways of dividing up the world and reject others may be
metaphysical, conventional, experiential, ... In analyzing arguments
we take the categories as we find them, leaving to metaphysicians or
scientists the task of revising the categories.

But what internal reasons are there for rejecting (*) in favor of Example 19? What can we tell from inspection of their forms and the meanings of their words? That's applying the wrong criterion. We have to use our knowledge of the world to evaluate generalizations.[8]

Thus, there are two substantial problems with using a principle of the uniformity of nature to justify our generalizations.

- It is less plausible than the conclusion of any generalization we want to justify.

- It requires that we have correctly described what is significant in the sample and population.

But these problems occur in every use of a large metaphysical principle in our reasoning, such as "There are things in the world" or "No claim is true or false." That is to say, we either accept a principle of uniformity as part of our metaphysics or we don't. We do not argue to it, and it would take one or many very clear examples of how it fails to convince us to abandon it—if we can make it clear enough to use.

It's right in the long run
Nicholas Rescher says:

> [Charles Sanders] Peirce and, succeeding him, Hans Reichenbach, took the logical candidate [for entry into justifying generalizing] to be the key principle of proportional induction—the principle which Peirce himself characterized as "quantitative induction," but which (following Reichenbach) is nowadays often referred to as the "straight rule" of statistical induction. The rule is formulated in the following precept:
>
>> When a certain percentage of a population *P* have in fact been observed to have a particular trait *T*, then adopt *this very value* as your answer to the question: "What proportion of the entire population *P* have trait *T*?"
>
> . . . Peirce (and Reichenbach later on) proposed to resolve this justificating [sic] problem [why this rule was justified] by arguing that we know, *a priori* and by demonstration on general principles alone, that statistical induction *must inevitably succeed* in its intended mission and is consequently justified.[9]

The rule will eventually succeed. In the long run. After enough observing. But as Rescher notes, there are serious problems.

First, the long run may be a lot longer than anything we'll ever encounter. You might think that's O.K., since generalizing is predicting correctly for us in the short run, as we never get to the long run. But the proportion may vary wildly in the short run, not approaching any "short run limit" either. As Hans Reichenbach noted,

> The case of convergence coming too late [given the finite duration of human life] amounts to the same thing as the case of nonconvergence, as far as human abilities are concerned.[10]

Second, we may reach the limit all right, but we'd never know that. As John W. Lenz says,

> One need not be a devotee of ordinary language to insist that it is strange . . . to say that the method of induction will, if possible, *find* limits. At least this sense of "find" in which one never knows [and never can know] that one has found that for which one looks.[11]

It's the best guess

Nicholas Rescher proposes the following:

> Consider a question of the form: "Are the *F*'s also *G*'s?" The situation here is akin to that of a multiple-choice examination, where one can respond:
>
> (1) Yes, all of them are.
> (2) Never—none of them are.
> (3) No, some are and some aren't.
> (4) Don't know; can't say.
>
> This pretty well exhausts the range of alternatives. Now when in fact *all* of the observed *F*'s (over a fairly wide range) are indeed *G*'s, our path seems relatively clear. Alternative 4 is not an answer—it is a mere evasion of the question, a response of last resort, to be given only when all else has failed us. Alternative 2 is *ex hypothesi* ruled out in the circumstances. The choice [is] between 1 and 3. And we naturally opt for the former. The governing consideration here is the matter of plausibility—specifically that of uniformity. For 1 alone extends the data in the most natural way, seeing that this response alone aligns the tenor of our general answer with the specific information we actually have in hand. It is, accordingly, this resolution that affords the "inductively appropriate" answer in the postulated circumstances. . . .
>
> But why not always opt for safety in answering our questions, systematically selecting the noncommittal pseudoalternative "none

of the above"? Why not decline risk of error and simply follow the
path of skepticism? The answer is simple: Nothing ventured, nothing
gained. The object of the cognitive enterprise is clearly to secure
truth (and not simply to avert error!).[12]

That is, accept the generalization for lack of better. He continues,

> Induction is a matter of obtaining the optimum truth-estimate in terms
> of the systematic best fit secured through plausibilistic cogency. Its
> aim is to provide an answer that we can responsibly maintain to be
> true, and this is not a matter of simply identifying whatever answer is
> most probable in the sense of the mathematical calculus of probabilities.
> Thus, if we draw at random an integer from the range 1 to 1,000, it is
> very likely that 555 will *not* result. But it is not an inductively
> acceptable answer to the question, "What number will be obtained"
> to respond, "Well, at any rate it won't be 555." An inductive
> "conclusion" must be offered with full assertive interest: it will not do
> to say something like, "Well, I can't (or won't) really commit myself,
> but such-and-such would be the safest bet." The truth-estimative
> mission characteristic of the inductive enterprise goes beyond any
> mere probabilism.[13]

Rescher lacks a general theory of inference and argument that are
needed to make sense of what he means by "systematic best fit secured
through plausibilistic cogency." His criteria of systematization[14]—
completeness, cohesiveness, consonance, etc.—depend on his choice of
logic. And then we are back to asking for a justification of his logic.

The method of sampling works
Donald C. Williams argues that it is not a valid argument with a general
principle that justifies generalizing. Rather, we can have confidence
that our samples are really representative:

> Given a fair-sized sample, then, from any population, with no further
> material information, we know logically that it very probably is one
> of those which match the population, and hence that very probably
> the population has a composition similar to that which we discern in
> the sample. This is the logical justification of induction.[15]

But as noted above, this view of sampling relies on some principle
like the law of large numbers or the idea that it's right in the long run,
both of which need as much justification as the method of generalizing.
And how we "know logically" is the issue.

Even more clearly, Roy Harrod says we can rely on sampling. He says that the only postulate necessary is:

Our experience as a whole is a fair sample.[16]

And this, according to him, is not known *a priori* or through a valid argument. But perhaps he has not thought of the black swans in Australia which showed that the generalization from experience of people in Europe in the fifteenth century to "All swans are white" is not good.

Confirmation of the conclusion
A. J. Ayer says,

We can agree with Professor Popper that it does not matter for our purpose how generalisations are arrived at. The question which concerns us is what makes them acceptable. And here I think we can say that the only ground there can be for accepting any generalisation is that statements which record observed facts are derivable from it.[17]

Here Ayer uses "generalisation" to mean any general claim, what might be the conclusion of what I call a generalization.

Ayer and Karl R. Popper seem to be saying that no reasoning by generalizing can be good; such reasoning never gives us good reason to believe the conclusion.[18] No reasoning can justify our accepting such general claims. All we can do is try to falsify them. No generalization will give us certainty (very close to certainty?) that the conclusion is true. So just view generalizing as a route to conjectures. We'll "more or less" believe these conjectures until they lead to a contradiction with "observed facts."

But we never thought that generalizing would give us certainty. We can interpret what Ayer says as pointing out that generalizing will give us some but not perfect reason to believe the conclusion.

Now if that reason is so imperfect that we shouldn't accept any generalization as strong, then we never have good reason to believe the conclusion of a generalization. Perhaps Ayer and Popper agree to that.[19] But they often act as if they believed the conclusions of generalizations. Perhaps they could take the line of the Pyrrhonist who says that he acts without belief.[20]

Take it or leave it
Consider the following generalization:

Every apple that anyone has ever seen detach naturally
from a tree has fallen downward when the weather was calm.
Therefore, any apple when detached naturally from a tree will
fall downward in calm weather.

There is good reason to believe the premise. If someone had seen an
apple fall upward or stay suspended, we think it would have been
reported. How, then, should we view the conclusion?

We have no reason to believe the conclusion false. So the choice is
between suspending judgment or believing the conclusion true.

It is not irrational to suspend judgment, just very cautious. One
can act by habit as if apples fall downward without ever committing to
some notion of truth. But if someone says he will suspend judgment on
the conclusion, we can infer that it isn't just this argument. He would
not accept the conclusion of any generalization.

So we ask him if he thinks the following argument is good:

All but a very, very few dogs in the U.S. bark.
President Obama has a dog.
So President Obama's dog barks.

If he says he would suspend judgment there, too, we can infer that he
doesn't accept any strong argument as giving reason to believe its
conclusion.

So we ask him if he thinks the following argument is good:

No dog hibernates.
Juney is a dog.
So Juney does not hibernate.

If he says "yes," then he has shown that he considers only valid
arguments suitable for drawing conclusions in reasoning. And then we
can ask him why he draws that line.

If he says "no," then we ask him if he accepts the premises as true.
If he says "yes," then we see that he will probably not accept any form
of reasoning as giving a reason to believe a conclusion; he is an
academic skeptic. Then the traditional reply can be put to him: What
makes you think no argument gives good reason to believe its conclusion? It must be a mystical insight, since he cannot reply with an
argument for that belief.[21]

If he says "no," we've got to find out why he does not accept one
of the premises. He might say that "No dog hibernates" is uncertain to

him because it would have to be proved by a generalization. In that case, we can be fairly sure he will accept only conclusions of arguments that are valid and whose premises are true by virtue of form and meaning. Or he won't accept *any* claim as true, except perhaps reports on his own feelings/sensations. He suspends judgment on all. That is, he is a Pyrrhonist. That is not irrational. Sextus Empiricus has described how a Pyrrhonist can act by habit without any beliefs.[22]

In the end, generalizing well seems to give us *some* reason to believe the conclusion. The question is how to quantify, how to measure the strength of a generalization. If we have some way, then we can place generalizations among strong arguments when the measure is high, and they are good or not accordingly as you accept that strong arguments can be good.

There is, indeed, a mathematical theory for measuring the strength of generalizations. It is based on the law of large numbers. In the world of mathematical abstractions that's correct, but whether it applies to experience is what we have considered. We might even view it a variation on the uniformity of nature principle.

So either you accept that generalizing can be an acceptable method of reasoning if done well, and follow that mathematical line when possible. Or else you reject it and concern yourself only with making conjectures, adopting a skeptical stance. This you can do even if you accept that some strong arguments can be good. You could draw the line of skepticism with generalizing.

Appendix Hempel's paradox of confirmation

Consider the following claim:

(i)   All ravens are black.

There are two ways we can understand this.

(ii)   All ravens up to this time are black.

That is, every raven that has been or exists now was or is black. We have excellent reason to believe this. Many people in many places and many times have reported seeing ravens, and all reports of those have said the ravens were black. This is about the best generalization we are likely to get for a population that is so widespread.

(iii)   All ravens up to this time and in the future are black.

We have the same evidence as for (ii). This is about as strong evidence as we can expect to get for a generalization into the future about so widespread a population. Whether we should consider it to be a strong generalization, and if strong whether a good argument is an issue discussed above.

In either case, Carl G. Hempel says we have a "paradox of confirmation" in establishing (i).[23] He points out that "All ravens are black" is logically equivalent to:

(iv)   All non-black things are not ravens.

And thus:

(*)   Anything that confirms one of (i) or (iv), confirms the other.

So if we find a black raven, that confirms both (i) and (iv) (the claim "This is a black raven" is some confirmation). But if we find a white telephone, that too confirms both (the claim "This is a white telephone" is some confirmation). This, he says, is paradoxical. How can a white telephone confirm that all ravens are black?

Hempel's resolution is to say that there is no paradox at all, just a psychological resistance on our part to recognizing that white telephones confirm (i) and black ravens confirm (iv). Since that doesn't seem compatible with our intuitions, let's ask how Hempel gets (*). He has three assumptions:

1. Confirmation is distinct from proof and can be partial.
2. "Whatever confirms (disconfirms) one of two equivalent sentences, also confirms (disconfirms) the other."[24]
       Here "equivalent" means logically equivalent in classical predicate logic.
3. The right way to formalize "All X are Y" in classical predicate logic is "For anything, if it is an X, then it is a Y."

Each of these I will show is wrong, at least for this kind of example. There is no paradox because what confirms (iv) does not confirm (i).

First, consider the idea of what Hempel calls "confirmation." He is thinking of the situation where a scientist takes a general claim as an hypothesis and looks for confirmation of it.[25] So there is a need for a logic of confirmation and degrees of confirmation.

But that's just to say that there is a need for a logic governing generalizing. We are far from accomplishing that, as the discussions in this essay show.[26] To understand confirmation is to understand generalizing: see "Models and Theories" in *Reasoning in Science and Mathematics* and "Explanations" in *Cause and Effect, Conditionals, Explanations* in this series.

For now, it is enough to say that "A confirms B" just means that if A is added to the premises of the argument we already have for B, then the argument is stronger. We have some standards for that, as described in the previous essays. Our only method of reasoning with generalizations is via the sample/population route. We have, at least for now, nothing better. And white telephones aren't in the population for "All ravens are black." So a white telephone does not confirm "All ravens are black."

Still, we seem to have a paradox because of (2) and (3). But (3) is wrong. Hempel does not give explicit standards of what constitutes a good formalization of an ordinary language claim or inference into classical predicate logic. But formalizing must respect informally valid inferences.

In proving "All ravens are black" we consider the population to be all ravens. That is, we assume that there has been or will be at least one raven. We should formalize (i) as:

(v) There is at least one raven, and given any thing, if it is a raven, then it is black.

And we should formalize (iv) as:

(vi) There is at least one thing that isn't black; and given any thing, if it is not black, then it is not a raven.

And (v) is not equivalent to (vi) when formalized in classical predicate logic.

However, given the assumption that there is at least one raven and there is at least one thing that isn't black, both of which are true, we do get that (v) is equivalent to (vi). So even noting that Hempel is wrong in the details, the apparent paradox remains.[27]

But why should we accept (2)? Hempel's main argument is that scientists reason that way. But that's false. Some small portion of how scientists reason can be formalized in classical predicate logic. But much cannot. When scientists want to establish a generalization, they clearly are not using (just) classical predicate logic, but some informal logic governing how to generalize well, a logic of arguments, what we have been trying to develop in these essays. We have a paradox only if we assume that classical predicate logic is the (only) right way to reason, which contradicts Hempel's own attempt to establish a logic governing generalizing.

NOTES

1. (p. 135) If the first object chosen was from that subgroup, then the chance of the second object being from that subgroup is actually slightly less than 14%. This account of sampling is necessarily simplified, but more precision would not affect the main points under discussion.

2. (p. 140) Charles Sanders Peirce, "A Theory of Probable Inference," p. 205 (*Collected Papers*, vol. 6.408).

3. (p. 140) See "Explanations" in *Cause and Effect, Conditionals, Explanations*.

4. (p. 141) C. S. Peirce, "A Theory of Probable Inference," p. 194.

5. (p. 143) This is part of the *problem of induction*. I do not use that phrase because discussions of the problem of induction typically conflate and confuse the following questions, each of which is dealt with separately in at least one of the essays in this series of volumes:

- How do we define "strong argument"?
- How do we define "induction"?
- How do we define "generalization"?
- Can a strong argument be good?
- Can a generalization be a strong argument?
- What is cause and effect?
- How can we reason about cause and effect?
- What is an explanation?
- What is a good explanation?

See, for example, A. J. Ayer's reconstruction of Hume's analysis in *Probability and Evidence*, pp. 4–6. L. Jonathan Cohen in *The Philosophy of Induction and Probability* §20 slips unaccountably from a discussion of evaluating evidence for generalizations to a method for testing causal hypotheses. G. H. von Wright gives an historical survey of the problem of induction in Chapter 1 of *A Treatise on Induction and Probability*, but despite taking induction initially to be reasoning from experience, he considers only the question of whether concluding a universal generalization from particular instances of it can be a good argument. A summary of the history of the problem of induction is in Max Black's "Induction." Ian Hacking in Chapter 19 of his *The Emergence of Probability* offers an historical explanation of why these questions were originally conflated. Kisor Kumar Chakrabarti in *Definition and Induction* shows how and why the question of whether a generalization can be good is discussed in terms of cause and effect in the classical Indian tradition.

.

6. (p. 146) This is the same problem encountered in the definitions and applications of probability discussed in "Probability" in this volume.

7. (p. 146) Chapters III and IV of *Fact, Fiction, and Forecast.* See L. Jonathan Cohen, *The Philosophy of Induction and Probability*, §25 for a survey of analyses of this example. In *Grue!*, Douglas Stalker, ed., some of the best-known analyses of (*) have been collected.

8. (p. 148) Nelson Goodman says in *Fact, Fiction, and Forecast*, p. 83:

> Our failures teach us, I think, that lawlike or projectible hypotheses cannot be distinguished on any merely syntactical grounds or even on the ground that these hypotheses are somehow purely general in meaning.

9. (p. 148) *Induction*, pp. 99–100.

10. (p. 149) *Experience and Prediction*, p. 361.

11. (p. 149) "Problems for the Practicalist's Justification of Induction," p. 100.

12. (p. 150) *Induction*, pp. 8–9.

13. (p. 150) Ibid., p. 27.

14. (p. 150) Ibid., p. 31.

15. (p. 150) *The Ground of Induction*, p. 97.

16. (p. 151) *Foundations of Inductive Logic*, p. 253. To paraphrase: All is for the most representative in this most representative of all possible worlds.

17. (p. 151) *Probability and Evidence*, p. 19.

18. (p. 151) See Karl R. Popper's late summing up of his views in "Conjectural Knowledge: My Solution of the Problem of Induction." There and elsewhere he seems to confuse the evaluation of generalizations with the evaluation of explanations.

19. (p. 151) Hume, *A Treatise of Human Nature*, Book I, Part III, Section 12, p. 139, certainly believed that generalizations can't be shown to justify belief:

> There is nothing in any object, consider'd in itself, which can afford us a reason for drawing a conclusion beyond it; and, That even after the observation of the frequent or constant conjunction of objects, we have no reason to draw any inference concerning any object beyond those of which we have had experience.

Francis Bacon, *Novum Organum*, i. 105, is more blunt:

> The induction which proceeds by simple enumeration is puerile, leads

to uncertain conclusions and is exposed to danger from one contradictory instance.

20. (p. 151) Hilary Putnam makes just this point in his "The 'Corroboration of
Theories'," Sections 1–3, especially as regards applications of generalizations
in science.

21. (p. 152) David Miller, *Critical Rationalism,* particularly Chapter 3 says
the best that reasoning can do is give us more reason to believe one claim
than another: No argument gives us good reason to believe its conclusion.
But the analyses of what counts as good reason to believe the conclusion of
an argument apply equally to there being more reason to believe one claim
than another.

22. (p. 153) See *The Skeptic Way: Sextus Empiricus's Outlines of
Pyrrhonism* by Benson Mates. See also "Rationality" in this volume.

23. (p. 154) "Studies in the Logic of Confirmation."

24. (p. 154) Ibid., p 13.

25. (p. 155) Hempel talks as if an hypothesis such as "All ravens are black" is
independent of how it is expressed, thereby assuming a realist metaphysics of
propositions. But that is not necessary for what he does, and I will not discuss
it here.

26. (p. 155) Hempel does make an attempt in "A Purely Syntactical Definition
of Confirmation," as do I in Chapter 9 of *Five Ways of Saying "Therefore."*

27. (p. 155) Hempel makes the following points in his "Studies in the Logic of
Confirmation" regarding the formalization of (i) as (v):

(a) *It doesn't allow the equivalence of* "All ravens are black" *with* "All
non-black things are ravens." But that is not a reason to reject this formalization, unless you think that finding an anomaly is good.

(b) *It's not customary.* He considers the claim "Anyone receiving a
particular skin injection who tests positive has diphtheria." He says we don't
have a clear notion of the sample here: Is it all people? All people who have
had an injection? All people who have had the injection and had a reaction?
There's no clear choice for what the existential assumption should be.

But there is: It's the last one. Moreover, it is in keeping with what
scientists do: They don't look at people who haven't had a skin injection
to confirm this claim.

(c) *Many universal hypotheses don't imply an existential clause.* He
gives as an example "Whenever man and ape are crossed, the offspring will
have such and such characteristics." He says,

Unquestionably, the hypothesis does not imply an existential clause asserting that the contemplated kind of cross-breeding referred to will, at some time, actually take place. (p. 17)

But we do not try to prove the claim by the standard methods of generalizing. Without any existing ape-human cross-breed, the claim is a counterfactual, "If there were an ape-human cross breed, it would have such and such characteristics," the analysis of which is quite different, as discussed in "Conditionals" in *Cause and Effect, Conditionals, Explanations*.

As further evidence that no existential clause should be included in the formalization of "All ravens are black," Hempel considers "All sodium salts burn yellow." We use this, he says, to show that something is not sodium by showing that it doesn't burn yellow. But we can use the formalization "There are such things as sodium salts, and for anything, if it's a sodium salt, it burns yellow" to the same end.

Hempel's discussion shows the importance of developing criteria for formalizing, which I do in *Predicate Logic*.

Probabilities

The usual notions of probability can sometimes be useful in inference analysis, but they are not adequate to make precise the notions of plausibility and likelihood of a possibility.

Three ways to understand "probably"

Example 1 Dick can't fit into a Mazda Miata sports car. Therefore:
  (1) Probably Dick is over 6 feet tall.

Analysis Is "probably" part of the conclusion (1) or a comment on it?

The frequentist view of probability says that a sentence that contains "probably," or "more likely," or "25% of the time" is true just in case the claim would be true with that frequency in a long run of trials. That makes sense for:

(2) There is a 1/6 chance of this die showing 1 on top if it is thrown.

It makes no sense at all for "Dick is over 6 feet tall."

The degree of belief view of probability holds that "probably" is a commentary on the claim "Dick is over 6 feet tall." It expresses the speaker's belief, the degree with which he or she would agree or bet that "Dick is over 6 feet tall" is true. The word "probably" isn't part of the conclusion of the example but only indicates the speaker's estimate of the strength of the inference.

The logical relation view is similar in that it takes "probably" to be a comment on the nature of the inference: It is more reasonable than not to believe "Dick is over 6 feet tall" is true. Then an explanation has to be given for what is reasonable to believe.

For some claims, such as (1), it is clear that the degree of belief or the logical relation view is correct. The frequentist view doesn't make sense.

For some claims, such as (2), the frequentist view seems better. On the degree of belief view we would have:

It seems 1/6 likely to me that "This die will show 1 on top if it is thrown" is true.

That substitutes a subjective claim for what is clearly intended to be an objective one.[1] On the logical relation view we would have:

It is 1/6 reasonable to believe that "This die will show 1 on top if it is thrown" is true.

That supposedly would be objective, but seems to miss the point that (2) is a prediction about the nature of the world, not a claim about belief or the role of a claim in reasoning.

Example 1 illustrates three ways to understand claims such as "Probably Dick is over 6 feet tall" or "Probably the die will show 1":

The *frequency* view
Words like "probably" are to be interpreted numerically as the proportion in the long run of how often the claim would be true in a series of trials.

The *degree of belief* view
The word "probably" indicates the speaker's belief about how likely the claim with that word deleted is true given the premises of the inference. Words like "probably" and "certainly" indicate the speaker's attitude.

The *logical relation* view
The sentence is the conclusion of an inference, and words like "probably" and "certainly" are not part of the claim but refer to how reasonable it is to believe the claim given the premises of the inference.

Each of these ways to understand "probably" is meant to generate the mathematical calculus of probabilities, as discussed below, when suitably interpreted.[2]

The logical relation view of probability

What are we measuring?
For some inferences we can assign a number measuring how likely it is that the conclusion is true given that the premises are true. For example:

(3) This die is well-made and perfectly regular.
Therefore, this die will show 1 when it is thrown.

We can say that the probability of the conclusion being true given this premise is exactly 1/6. How do we measure?

On this view, to assign a number to an inference we need to calculate the ratio:

(4) $$\frac{\text{number of ways that the premises could be true and conclusion true}}{\text{number of ways that the premises could be true}}$$

But there will always be a potentially infinite number of ways the world could be such that the premises are true.[3] For example, we can add that Caesar was born 1 second later, or 1.00001 seconds later, or . . . if the date of his birth is irrelevant to the premises and conclusion, in the sense that assuming the added premise does not change whether the conclusion is true in that description. So the ratio (4) cannot be a number.

How, then, can we assign 1/6 to inference (3)? We draw equivalences. We say that every claim other than the following is irrelevant:

(5) The die will show 1.
The die will show 2.
The die will show 3.
The die will show 4.
The die will show 5.
The die will show 6.

That is, the only aspect of the way the world could be that matters in judging the likelihood that the conclusion is true given the premises are true is which of the six claims at (5) is true. We have six equivalence classes of the ways the world could be, defined by these six claims.

But we need more. We need that each of those classes has the same number of possible ways. That's what the premise of (4) is meant to guarantee. So we have six equal classes. The conclusion is true in just one of them. Hence, there is a 1/6 chance that the conclusion is true given that the premise is true. To give a definition of how to assign a number to the strength of an inference, we must explain what is meant by "each class has the same number of possible ways."

The Principle of Indifference

Prior to John Maynard Keynes the analysis of probability was typically based on a Principle of Indifference.[4] Here is how he describes it:

> The Principle of Indifference asserts that if there is no *known* reason
> for predicating of our subject one rather than another of several
> alternatives, then relatively to such knowledge the assertions of
> each of these alternatives have an *equal* probability. Thus *equal*
> probabilities must be assigned to each of several arguments, if there
> is an absence of positive ground for assigning *unequal* ones.[5]

Keynes criticized the use of the Principle of Indifference as giving paradoxical results because it cannot distinguish "good" descriptions from "bad" ones:

> If, for instance, having no evidence relevant to the colour of this
> book, we could conclude that 1/2 is the probability of 'This book is
> red,' we could conclude equally that the probability of each of the
> propositions 'This book is black' and 'This book is blue' is also 1/2.
> So that we are faced with the impossible case of *three* exclusive
> alternatives all as likely as not. A defender of the Principle of
> Indifference might rejoin that we are assuming knowledge of the
> proposition: 'Two different colours cannot be predicated of the same
> subject at the same time'; and that, if we know this, it constitutes
> relevant outside evidence. But such evidence is about the predicate,
> not about the subject. Thus the defender of the Principle will be
> driven on, either to confine it to cases where we know nothing about
> either the subject or the predicate, which would be to emasculate it
> for all practical purposes, or else to revise and amplify it, which is
> what we propose to do ourselves.[6]

Keynes' repair of the Principle of Indifference is first to define what it means for a claim A to be irrelevant to another B given other claims $C_1, C_2, \ldots$ as premises in terms of the probability of B given $C_1, C_2, \ldots$ compared to B given both A and $C_1, C_2, \ldots$. But he returns again and again to concerns about whether the descriptions we give are "indivisible alternatives."[7]

A definition of "probability"
Here is a definition of a measure of the probability that the premises of an inference could be true and the conclusion false at the same time.

Probabilities and Possibilities (PP)

Given an inference, if there is no way that the premises could be true, or if every way that the premises are true the conclusion is too (the inference is valid), then the probability of the conclusion being true given that the premises are true is 1. If there is some way the premises could be true and no way the conclusion could be true, the probability is 0. Otherwise, the probability is numerically calculable if and only if:

   i. We have a collection of n claims $C_1, C_2, \ldots, C_n$
       such that no two can be true at the same time, and for
       any possible way the premises could be true, there is
       a description of it that includes one of these.

   ii. The conclusion of the inference is true if and only if at
       least one of $C_{i_1}, C_{i_2}, \ldots, C_{i_m}$ is true, where $0 < m < n$.

   iii. If there is a description of a way the premises could be
        true that includes C_i, then we can replace C_i by any
        other C_j to get a description of another way the premises
        could be true.

In this case the ***probability*** is m/n.[8] If the probability is not numerically calculable, the strength of the inference is ***imprecise***.

Given two inferences with the same premises and different conclusions, the conclusions are ***equiprobable*** relative to those premises if they have the same numerical probability.

The purport of (i) and (ii) is that the claims $C_1, C_2, \ldots, C_n$ divide up all possible ways the premises could be true into mutually exclusive classes, in m of which the conclusion is true. Condition (iii) is a way to formalize the idea that the classes given by $C_1, C_2, \ldots C_n$ are equinumerous.[9]

Example 2 This die is well-made and perfectly regular. Therefore, this die will show 1 or 2 when it is thrown.

Analysis The analysis proceeds as for inference (3), using the six claims at (5). The conclusion is true in two of the six classes determined by these claims, so the probability is 1/3 .

This division according to the six classes at (5) is an abstraction: We ignore the possibilities that the cube could end up perched on an edge or be swallowed by a passing bird. We say those outcomes "don't count." Calculating probabilities depends on what we take to be a possible way the premises could be true (an outcome of an experiment). It is not an observation about the world that there are six possible outcomes, but a rule that we will only notice ways that the world could be that fall into one of those classes.

In this case, the measure of the strength of the inference can be calculated because we built that into the inference with the premise. If it's a new die that's never been used, we have good reason to believe that premise. But if we knew that the die had been used for a month at a casino and discarded, we would have less reason to believe the premise. And if we had seen the die come up "4" fifteen of the last eighteen times it was rolled, we'd have much less reason to believe the premise.

Instead of the six claims we used to analyze (3) why don't we use thirty-six claims: "The die will show *n* after having been immediately previously on side *m*"? To do so would require the additional premise that a die never lands solidly on just one side without turning at least once (this is a rule in games of chance using dice in casinos). Then we could consider those thirty-six classes instead of the six, and the calculations of probabilities would turn out the same.

Definition (PP) does not say that there is only one class of claims we can use to calculate probabilities, as we saw in the last example. Suppose we have an inference and two different collections of claims for which (PP) apply, say $C_1, C_2, \ldots, C_n$, for *m* of which the conclusion is true, and $D_1, D_2, \ldots, D_s$, for *r* of which the conclusion is true. To use (PP) we should show that $m/n = r/s$. I cannot see how to do that unless, as in the last example, the classes given by the D_i's are refinements (subclasses) of those given by the C_j's. This is the problem that Keynes and others point out with the Principle of Indifference: we cannot guarantee that we have the "right" description of the world. We can only stipulate.

Determining the strength of an inference is relative to our beliefs. That includes our beliefs about the right way to divide up descriptions of the world. If some ways of dividing up all possibilities are right and some wrong, beyond some satisfying (PP) and some not, then there may be just one correct calculation of probabilities. At present we have no way to determine that. What we do have is a formalization of how we do go about determining the strength of an inference: we make certain idealizations or abstractions that satisfy (PP) and calculate.[10]

Example 3   *a*. This die is well-made and perfectly regular.
            Therefore, this die will show 1 when it is thrown.

            b. This die is well-made and perfectly regular.
            Therefore, this die will show 2 when it is thrown.

Analysis   The analysis proceeds as for inference (3), showing that the two conclusions are equiprobable: each has probability 1/6 *relative to the same premise.*

Example 4   A card is drawn from a deck.
            Therefore, the card is a heart.

Analysis   Suppose someone suggests there are two classes for this analysis, C_1 "It is a heart" and C_2 "It is not a heart," so that the probability of the premise being true and conclusion false is 1/2.

That is not a correct application of (PP). The two classes defined by the claims "It is a heart" and "It is not a heart" satisfy conditions (i) and (ii) of (PP) but not (iii). One way the premise could be true, for example, is if "The card is a 2 and it is a heart" is part of the description, in which case C_1 is true. But if we replace "It is a heart" with "It is not a heart" we do not get a unique description of a way the world could be that satisfies C_2, for the card could be the 2 of diamonds, the 2 of clubs, or the 2 of spades.

A way to satisfy (PP) is to have 52 classes, one for each particular card in the deck; in 13 of those "It is a heart" appears, so the probability is $13/52 = 1/4$. But even then is condition (iii) satisfied? Suppose the description of the world is very detailed, including a claim that describes the exact order or the cards in the deck after it has been shuffled and which card, starting from the top of the deck, is drawn, say the 27th. You might think we can't replace "It is 2 and is a heart" with any other of the 52 claims to get a new description of a possibility in which the premises are true because the description forces just this one. But we could, for we don't change just "It is 2 and is a heart" with, say, "It is 7 and is a spade" but also the part of the description of the order of the cards in the deck, so when we come to "The 27th card is a 2 and is a heart" we have instead "The 27th card is a 7 and is a spade".

The purport of condition (iii) is that our descriptions are meant to be indifferent to which of $C_1, C_2, \ldots, C_n$ is included. If we find a description that can't be varied in such a way, we have chosen to pay attention to more than just the possibility that one of these n claims is true.

Example 5   This die is loaded to make 1 show up more often.
Therefore, this die will show 1 when it is thrown.

Analysis   Previously we had a premise "The die is fair," which just means we have good reason to believe that any description in one of the six classes at (3) is a description in every other of the classes if just the defining claim is varied.

We have a new premise: "The die is loaded to make 1 show up more often." This means that we have reason to believe that a description of how the world could be which includes "The die shows 1" would not necessarily be a description of how the world could be if we replaced that with "The die shows 2." If we knew exactly how the die was loaded and had a better grasp of the physics involved, we could isolate differences in the descriptions of possible ways the premises could be true. Then isolating those differences in terms of particular claims, we could, perhaps, say exactly how many different classes there are in establishing an equivalence relation on possible ways. That is, we could calculate a numerical probability for "The die shows 1" is true given the premises.

Perhaps an engineer would estimate a probability for "The die shows 1" based on what she knew. But unless she makes explicit her assumptions, her estimate is only a guess, not a calculation of probability on this view.

Example 6   D. J. Watling in an article entitled "Confirmation Discomforted" asks [us] to suppose that "we are following a man along a road and reach a place where the road divides into three, two paths climbing the hillside, one lying in the valley". Knowing nothing but that the man, now out of sight, will take one of the three paths, how are we to estimate the probability that he will take the path lying in the valley? If we regard all three paths as equally possible, we shall estimate it as 1/3 , but we might just as well regard his going into the hills and his going into the valley as being equally possible, in which case it would be 1/2. This does not show the method to be inconsistent, since we can always take measures to ensure consistency. In this instance, we have antecedently to make a ruling which will direct which procedure we are to follow. Even so, it appears unsatisfactory that different methods of ensuring consistency should lead to markedly different results, and that the decision between them should be wholly arbitrary.[11]

Analysis A. J. Ayer presents this example as illustrating the problem that how we assign probabilities depends on how we carve up all possibilities.[12]

According to (PP) we cannot assign a precise probability to the conclusion "The man will go along this path" given the description (premises) of the example. We have no reason to think—as Ayer tells us—that given any way in which both the premises and "The man goes into the valley" are true is also a description of how the premises could be true if we replace the latter claim with "The man goes up the hillside." We cannot take "measures to ensure consistency" if we don't know anything more than what he says. There is no reason to think that a numerical probability can always be assigned: any assignment of the numerical strengths here is arbitrary.

It is not clear that any two divisions of classes that satisfy (PP) will result in the same numerical probability. Our divisions are relative to the ways we think the world can be described, which in turn may be relative to our beliefs. It may also be relative to what we choose to ignore in our (potential) experience, to what we pay attention to in our reasoning.

The frequency view of probability

The frequency view takes words like "probably" to be part of the claim. On that reading "There is a 1/6 chance the die will show 1" is meant as either a forecast or a statement of fact about possibilities: in the long run the proportion of times a fair die will show 1 when thrown will be 1/6. Here "in the long run" means that the more trials that are done, the closer the proportion of times the die will show 1 will approach to 1/6 (the *frequency* will approach 1/6). But what is a trial?

Suppose we want to say that in the long run the frequency of choosing a 2 of spades from a deck of cards is 1/52. Suppose we do trials. Well, after 50,000 trials the deck would be so mangled we wouldn't be getting 1/52 anymore. So what does "in the long run" mean? It can't be *actual* trials. It must be *possible* trials—and then the frequency view devolves into the possibility definition of probability (PP) given above.

Suppose instead that the trials were done to show that the frequency probability of drawing a 2 of spades from a new deck of cards is 1/52. We could do a lot of trials, maybe 50,000 or more, each with a new deck, and find that the frequency does approach 1/52. But what reason do we have for assuming that it will continue? Maybe new decks of cards will be made differently in the future. Our belief will depend on either a strong assumption that the world will continue to be the same, or assumptions about the nature of decks of cards. And the latter (surely preferable) is just how we would go about giving the possibility analysis of probability, the assumptions being built into the descriptions of the ways the premises could be true.

Suppose we flipped one penny 10,000 times and found that the frequency that heads showed was close to 1/2. That wouldn't give us a frequency reason for thinking the same holds for another penny. To get that, we'd need an argument whose strength, it seems, would depend on a possibility analysis of probability.[13]

Perhaps we could say that frequency really isn't about the relation of premises to conclusion but gives a probability of the conclusion by itself, a statement of mathematics applied to experience. Given the way the world is, this is the probability. But that's just to say that the premises are not made explicit in favor of talk about "the way the world is." There may be an objective, non-arbitrary measure of the frequency of an "event" in a long run of trials, or even of the likelihood that an event will occur, a measure that is part of the nature of the world. That would be, perhaps, what is meant by "objective chance."[14] However, no one has offered a way for us to find those numbers.

What we have are projections from finite trials, based on an assumption that the world will pretty much continue as it has in the past. Or we have that the notion of a trial is really that of a possibility, and this view of probability becomes a subspecies of the logical relation view.

The subjective degree of belief view of probability

A particular notion of degree of belief has been developed by Frank
P. Ramsey, Bruno de Finetti, and L. J. Savage in an attempt to make
judgments about plausibility and likelihood precise and susceptible
to a mathematical theory.[15]

Suppose Dick is asked to make a number of judgments of values
for the plausibility of claims or the strength of inferences. Dick may
say that, given what he knows about Suzy, there's a 1/3 chance she'll
pass her critical thinking course, and a 1/4 chance she'll not pass the
course.

Ramsey and others would say that Dick's judgments are unreasonable or incoherent. They say we should only pay attention to estimates
made by a "rational" person. Dick should be willing to adjust his
assignments so that he doesn't assign values in such a way that, were
he to bet according to them, he would lose no matter what the outcome
(that is, a *Dutch book* could be made against him). Here Maria could
exploit Dick's assignments by betting 2 to 1 that Suzy will pass, and 3
to 1 that she will not pass. Then if Suzy passes, Dick loses $1, while if
she doesn't pass, Dick loses $2. We can use subjective degree of belief
assignments as a basis of probability only if we consider judgments
made by people who are *idealized gamblers*.[16]

Though the numerical assignments made by each reasoner who
is an idealized gambler satisfy the mathematical laws of probability
(described below), those assignments may vary wildly from one
reasoner to another. Yet as more evidence is accumulated the estimates
should converge, on the further assumption that the reasoner adjusts his
estimates according to Bayes' Theorem.[17] As Max Black says,

> Since the prior probabilities entering into the calculations are
> supposed to reflect only the varying *opinions* of different reasoners,
> it might be thought that no generally acceptable estimates of the
> strength of given evidence could result. De Finetti, however, relies
> upon the asymptotically diminishing effect of such varying assign-
> ments of initial probabilities as empirical evidence accumulates. He
> is able to show, in effect, that in a large number of interesting cases
> the choices made of the initial probabilities have, in the long run,
> negligible influence on the conclusions of statistical inference.[18]

So an engineer could make estimates of how likely it is that a
loaded die will show 1 when thrown, and then, adjusting her estimates

according to evidence she gets from additional throws, obtain probabilities that grow closer and closer to those made by another engineer starting with a different estimate.

Or an engineer could estimate how likely it is that a bridge he's designing will fail within 5 years. Another engineer could make a different estimate. But then how could either accumulate additional empirical evidence that could lead their estimates to converge?

Can probability theory provide a foundation for inference analysis?

The mathematical theory of probabilities is characterized by the following axioms, where P stands for a function from claims (alternatively, sets of "events" or "trials") to the real numbers, and A, B stand for claims (collections of events):

1. $0 \leq P(A) \leq 1$.

2. $P(B) = 1 - P(A)$ where B is a contradictory of A (B is the set-theoretic complement of A).

3. If $P(A \text{ and } B) = 0$, then $P(A \text{ or } B) = P(A) + P(B)$ (if $P(A \cap B) = 0$, then $P(A \cup B) = P(A) + P(B)$).

4. If A and B are equivalent in the classical propositional calculus, then $P(A) = P(B)$.

The three interpretations of "probably" described above are each meant to generate this mathematical calculus of probabilities. Should we replace our intuitive notion of likelihood or plausibility with one of them?

Transitivity
Probability is transitive: If A is more probable than B, and B is more probable than C, then A is more probable than C. But plausibility is not transitive.

Dick prefers strawberry ice cream to chocolate, and chocolate ice cream to vanilla. But he also prefers vanilla ice cream to strawberry. Dick asks Zoe for ice cream for dessert, and as she goes to the freezer she considers three claims:

A Dick would like strawberry ice cream tonight.
B Dick would like chocolate ice cream tonight.
C Dick would like vanilla ice cream tonight.

She knows Dick well, and she finds A more plausible than B, B more plausible than C, but C more plausible than A. There is nothing irrational, incoherent, or absurd about this. Moreover, we can convert these plausibility rankings into rankings of the strength of inferences with premise "Dick wants ice cream tonight" and conclusions A, B, and C.

One colleague pointed out that businessmen routinely impose the requirement of transitivity in mathematically modeling consumer demand. Does that mean they use a different notion of plausibility? Plausibility often is transitive, and when it is, one of the three interpretations might be suitable. But when we find a situation in which plausibility isn't transitive, probability cannot take its place. If Zoe finds only two kinds of ice cream in the freezer, she'll know which one to serve Dick. But if she finds all three, she'll have to go and ask Dick which he wants. We can and often need to investigate how plausible one claim is compared to two, three, or more claims, rather than just one.

Supposing that we restrict ourselves to situations in which plausibility is transitive, can one of the interpretations of probability serve as a foundation of inference analysis?

The logical relation view

This view was designed to reflect our intuitive analyses of the strength of inferences. For some arguments, such as those involving games of chance, we can give a numerical measure to the strength of an inference. As codified in (PP), those numerical probabilities satisfy the mathematical theory of probability if we add to that theory:

> A and B are any claims evaluated relative to the same collection of premises for which the two arguments have numerical probabilities.

However, for many inferences we have no way to calculate or assign a numerical measure according to the logical relation view, not just in practice, but even in theory.[19] The logical relation view does not appear to provide a foundation for making precise the notion of plausibility/likelihood except in those cases where we make sufficient assumptions about what we will pay attention to in our reasoning to allow us to calculate numerical probabilities.

The frequency view

Even were an objective, non-arbitrary measure of chance available to us, it would not apply to the vast majority of inferences we wish to analyze. Consider:

> Almost all dogs bark
> Ralph is a dog
> So Ralph barks

This is not about the frequencies of choosing dogs from a collection, since "almost all dogs" is meant, typically, as almost all dogs that exist now, or in the past, or in the future. Even if restricted to only dogs living now, it is hard to see how a frequency view of probability could help us analyze the strength of the inference. But perhaps it might, relative to our background assumptions, which we could try to make explicit, and that elusive objective measure. But we don't know what percentage of dogs bark—nor does it seem likely we could. We use "almost all" because we want to be imprecise.

It does not seem that the frequency view of probability can provide a foundation for inference analysis.

The degree of belief view

The most promising candidate for a foundation of inference analysis would seem to be the subjective degree of belief view. But as Max Black says (where I would talk of a good reasoner rather than a rational person):

> It is not clear why the desire to prevent others from "making a Dutch book" against oneself should be regarded as a necessary criterion of rationality, to be accepted without further ado. It might be objected that to be willing to accept simultaneous bets for and against a certain outcome at the same stakes (and thus to be as coherent as subjectivists require) would be to destroy the point of betting by ensuring that no money would change hands. It is only bookmakers, who are bound to accept a variety of bets on both sides of a given outcome, who need fear a "Dutch book." And even they, like traders in foreign exchange, are not to be counted as irrational in buying at a lower price than that at which they would sell. In any case, behavior that is prudent for bookmakers seems an inadequate basis for an analysis of rationality in general. A man would not be irrational if he insisted on betting on only one side of a question; nor would he necessarily be irrational if he offered odds of 1:3 on *H* and 1:2 on [not-*H*], with the stipulation that wagers on *H* must be at least three times as large as those on [not-*H*].[20]

Ramsey, however, defends the gambling viewpoint:

> These are the laws of probability, which we have proved to be necessarily true of any consistent set of degrees of belief. Any definite set of degrees of belief which broke them would be inconsistent in the sense that it violated the laws of preferences between options, such as that preferability is a transitive asymmetrical relation, and that if α is preferable to β, β for certain cannot be preferable to α if p, β if not-p. If anyone's mental condition violated these laws, his choice would depend on the precise form in which the options were offered him, which would be absurd. He could have a book made against him by a cunning bettor, and would then stand to lose in any event.[21]

But what is absurd about our preferences depending on how options are offered to us? This is a commonplace observation established by psychologists.

To assume that someone you are reasoning with is an idealized gambler goes far beyond the assumptions we make in reasoning with others.[22] Many people simply don't bet, or won't bet, or have no idea how to bet. Should someone who is unwilling to bet for religious reasons automatically be classified as a bad reasoner? Should a good background in horse racing and five-card stud be a necessary background for learning logic? With time we can tell if someone is a good reasoner, but we can't tell if a person is even a marginally competent gambler if he or she refuses to bet. Betting isn't an essential notion in the analysis of arguments, and it certainly isn't one on which we want to build our theory of argument analysis.

Conclusion

Each of the three views of probability seems inadequate as a foundation of argument analysis, though each seems perfectly apt when our reasoning can be put in a mathematical form compatible with the assumptions of that view. But those assumptions not only differ, they yield different calculations of probability.[23]

It is not just that assigning numbers to the plausibility of claims or the strength of inferences would often be arbitrary or depend on the particular interpretation of probability. Enforcing the assignment of numbers would in many cases pervert the inherent vagueness of these notions. Compare the quantifier "most": Gila Sher gives a precise mathematical interpretation of it as "a majority of."[24] Whatever we mean by "most" it certainly isn't that. I would not say that most birds in a flock just flew away if one less than half are still in the tree; I would not say a professor failed most of her students if she failed 37 of the 73 students in her class. The point of using "most" in a claim or inference is its vagueness, and to identify it with a mathematical operator gives some clear mathematics but is pointless as a guide to reasoning well. Someone could say, "So much the worse for that vague, imprecise reasoning. We should do away with it." But vagueness, imprecision, and judgment in our reasoning do not entail that we cannot give standards for how to reason well, as I try to show in the essays in this volume and in this series of books.

NOTES

1. (p. 162) See "Subjective Claims" in this volume for a definition of "subjective claim."

2. (p. 163) The logical relation view is often called the *degree of confirmation* view or *objective degree of belief* view. The idea of a degree of confirmation was developed in the context of analyzing explanations, but the analysis of the inference relation need not be in that context only. The term "objective degree of belief" seems odd: what is intended is the degree of belief one should have based on some objective criteria. But that assumes that the logical relation analysis always, or at least usually results in objective evaluations. If belief is the issue, we have the degree of belief view.

Rudolf Carnap is one whose analysis of probability is tied primarily to explanations in *Logical Foundations of Probability*. His probability$_2$ corresponds, I believe, to the frequency view I describe. It is not clear to me that his probability$_1$ corresponds to the logical relation view.

Georg Henrik von Wright has a short historical survey and analysis of these views in Chapter 7.1 of *A Treatise on Induction and Probability*. See also L. Jonathan Cohen, *The Philosophy of Induction*.

3. (p. 163) In making this observation I am not supposing that there are some abstract objects called "possible ways." See the discussion in "Arguments."

4. (p. 164) Much of the discussion in this chapter is amplified in Keynes, *Treatise of Probability*, especially his Chapters III and IV. My definition of "probability," however, is not his.

5. (p. 164) Keynes, *A Treatise on Probability*, p. 42.

6. (p. 164) Ibid., p. 43. William Kneale goes further in *Probability and Induction*:

> That principle [of indifference], which purports to provide a rule for the determination of probabilities *a priori* from the consideration of our own ignorance, must be rejected entirely. Probability statements may be modest assertions, but even so they cannot be justified by mere ignorance. p. 149

This criticism, however, would lead to rejecting any reasoning by strong inferences, a consequence Kneale is apparently not willing to accept.

7. (p. 165) *A Treatise on Probability*, p. 55:

> The simplest definition of Irrelevance is as follows: h_1 is irrelevant to x on evidence h, if the probability of x on evidence hh_1 is the same as its probability on evidence h. But . . . theoretically

preferable [is]: h_1 is irrelevant to x on evidence h, if there is no
proposition inferrible from $h_1 h$ but not from h such that its
addition to evidence h affects the probability of x.

J. L. Mackie in *Truth, Probability, and Paradox* also makes probability
an epistemic notion. In talking of drawing a card from a deck he says:

> The mere fact that we know nothing that would lead us to expect one
> card rather than another to appear commits us to dividing our expecta-
> tions equally between the fifty-two. What makes this type of situation
> suitable for the application of the principle of indifference is just that it
> contains a set of alternatives similarly related to our knowledge and
> ignorance, *not* that these alternatives occur with equal frequency in
> long runs of tests. pp. 163

8. (p. 165) Someone who believes that possible worlds exist as abstract
objects can reformulate these conditions in terms of the claims C_i being
true in the world.

9. (p. 165) Bernard Bolzano had a similar conception of probability in his
Theory of Science, Part II, Chapter 3, Section 161 (pp. 240–241):

> Let the probability of a proposition M be relative to a premise A,
> namely that Caius has drawn a ball from an urn in which, among
> others, there is a ball numbered 1 and another numbered 2. I claim
> that, if no other premises are given, the following two propositions:
> 'Caius has drawn ball no. 1' and 'Caius has drawn ball no. 2' both
> have exactly the same degree of probability provided that the ideas
> 'no. 1' and 'no. 2' are among those which are envisaged as variable
> in the context of this enquiry. For if we compare these propositions
> with the given premise A, we notice that both of them have exactly
> the same relation to A, since the only difference between them is that
> one of them has the idea 'no. 1' where the other has the idea 'no. 2'.
> Both of these ideas are contained in the proposition A in one and the
> same way (namely without ranking, merely as a sum).

Theodore Hailperin discusses Bolzano's ideas in *Sentential Probability Logic*,
pp. 84–91.

10. (p. 167) P. F. Strawson notes this, too, in *Introduction to Logical Theory*
pp. 243–244, from which much of this discussion comes.

Bruno de Finetti in "Foresight: Its logical laws, its subjective sources"
says:

> It can then be shown that when we have events for which we know a
> subdivision into possible cases that we judge to be equally probable,
> the comparison between their probabilities can be reduced to the

purely arithmetic comparison of the ratio between the number of
favorable cases and the number of possible cases (not because the
judgment then has objective value, but because everything substantial
and thus subjective is already included in the judgment that the cases
constituting the division are equally probable). p. 101

11. (p. 169) A. J. Ayer, *Probability and Evidence,* pp. 35. The following
discussion refers to that and the succeeding pages. The article by D. J. Watling
is "Confirmation Discomforted," *Revue Internationale de Philosophie*, vol.
XVII, 1963, pp. 155-170.

12. (p. 169) Ayer actually says the problem is how we divide up the world into
predicates. But we might have an inference to which neither predicate logic nor
Aristotelian logic apply.

13. (p. 170) J. M. Keynes in *A Treatise of Probability* speaks similarly:

So far from Induction's lending support to the fundamental rules of
probability, it is itself dependent on them. In any case, it is generally
agreed that an inductive conclusion is only probable, and that its
probability increases with the number of instances upon which it is
founded. According to the frequency theory, this belief is only
justified if the majority of inductive conclusions actually are true,
and it will be false, even on our existing data, that *any* of them are
probable, if the acknowledged possibility that a majority are false is
an actuality. Yet what possible reason can the frequency theory offer,
which does not beg the question, for supposing a majority *are true*?
And failing this, what ground have we for believing the inductive
process to be reasonable? Yet we invariably assume that with our
existing knowledge it is reasonable to attach some weight to the
inductive method, even if future experience shows that *not one* of its
conclusions is verified in fact. The frequency theory, therefore, in its
present form at any rate, entirely fails to explain or justify the most
important source of the most usual arguments in the field of probable
inference. p. 107

But A. J. Ayer in *Probability and Evidence,* pp. 30–33 shows that Keynes'
attempt to found induction on probability also fails. See also the discussion of
the principle of the uniformity of nature in "Generalizing" in this volume.

14. (p. 170) See "Reasoning about cause and effect" in *Cause and Effect,
Conditionals, Explanations* for a discussion of objective chance in the analysis
of cause and effect.

15. (p. 171) See for example, Ramsey, *The Foundation of Mathematics and
Other Logical Essays*, de Finetti, "Foresight: Its Logical Laws, Its Subjective

Sources" and "Sul Significato Soggettivo della Probabilità," and Savage, *The Foundations of Statistics*. Maria Carla Galavotti says in "The Notion of Subjective Probability in the Work of Ramsey and de Finetti,"

> Ramsey and de Finetti . . . regard the notion of probability as only explicable in psychologistic terms, and think that it can only acquire a precise meaning through an operational definition. In other words, in order to give probability some meaning, a way of measuring it has to be specified. p. 242

16. (p. 171) De Finetti claims to give a basis for subjective probabilities that does not involve the notion of gambling in his "Foresight: Its Logical Laws, Its Subjective Sources." But that seems to be no different from the definition I gave, couched in terms of events rather than claims; see the quote in footnote 10 above.

17. (p. 171) We define $P(X/Y) = P(X \text{ and } Y) / P(Y)$. Then given a claim A and new evidence E, new assignments are made in accord with the formula: $P(A/E) = [P(E/A) \cdot P(A)] / P(E)$. See for example, Elliott Sober, "Epistemology for empiricists."

18. (p. 171) Max Black, "Probability," p. 477.

19. (p. 173) See pp. 17–18 and p. 9 of "Arguments" in this volume.

20. (p. 174) "Probability," p. 477.

21. (p. 177) Ramsey, *The Foundations of Mathematics and Other Logical Essays*, p. 182.

22. (p. 175) See the discussion of the Principle of Rational Discussion and the Mark of Irrationality in "Arguments" and in "Rationality" in this volume.

23. (p. 175) See "Probability and Decision" by Henry Kyburg, p. 62.

24. (p. 175) *The Bounds of Logic*, items (61) and (63) on p. 29 formalizing (36) and (38).

Rationality

Except for a clear minimal notion of rationality the use of that term is too vague to be helpful and can be replaced with other common terms that are clearer. Generally, the ascription of rationality or irrationality is a value judgment and not a tool of analysis.

"He's just irrational to say that." "She's acting irrationally." "That tribe holds irrational beliefs." "Scientists are eminently rational, and the perfect scientist would be the perfectly rational person."

Many discussions of reasoning and descriptions of people or peoples invoke some notion of rationality. It would seem that such a notion is central to those discussions. Yet rarely is "rational" defined or explained.[1]

Beliefs

Rationality is connected with beliefs. Even when behavior is deemed rational or irrational, it is because of some relation the behavior has to beliefs. There are at least three broad notions of belief that lead to different notions of rationality.

Conscious belief: a consciously held attitude to a claim
A conscious belief occurs when someone (or something?) thinks consciously that a particular claim is true. So right now Desidério Murcho believes that Cedar City is in the United States (I just asked him).[2]

Even assuming that a person continues to hold once-conscious beliefs, a person can hold only a small number of them.

Nonlinguistic belief

If we wish to ascribe belief to, say, dogs, then, since we have no evidence that dogs have a language or any notion of claim, we must understand belief in some other sense. It is unclear to me what exactly that other sense is.[3]

Such beliefs are typically inferred from the behavior of animals, but it is not clear whether there must be something more than the behavior to count as a belief. Perhaps a disposition to a behavior of a certain kind is meant. But typically those who discuss such beliefs speak of the thoughts of the animals.[4]

It is not clear that there are nonlinguistic beliefs. Some say there are not.[5] In any case, they would not be connected to reasoning in any straightforward way.

Dispositional beliefs

If someone says that he or she believes a claim, then we have good evidence that they would assent to that claim in the future, barring new circumstances they encounter that might make them change their mind. So we would have good evidence that a person has a particular dispositional belief, too.

On the other hand, let us call someone's dispositional belief that is not and has never been a conscious belief of that person a *purely dispositional belief.* Are there purely dispositional beliefs?

The only evidence we have for them is behavioral, since we cannot introspect them: once we think of the claim, the belief is conscious. That is, one can ascribe a particular purely dispositional belief only to other people, not to oneself. One might, though, say of oneself, "I have purely dispositional beliefs, I just can't point to any particular one." But we would know that about ourselves only by inferring from our past behavior or from a similarity of ourselves to others to whom we ascribe dispositional beliefs. Indeed, we think that a person can hold an infinity of such beliefs, limited only by their complexity and the fertility of our imagination in ascribing beliefs to someone who has never thought of them.

Let's now examine different notions of rationality corresponding to these distinct kinds of belief.

Conscious rationality for reasoning

I take it that if someone recognizes that an argument is good, then it is irrational for him or her to believe the conclusion is false.[6]

But is it rational to believe an argument is good and suspend judgment on the conclusion? Such skepticism should be applied thoroughly, not just to the conclusion. If one accepts that there is good reason to believe the premises of an argument, and that the argument is valid or strong, and that the premises are more plausible than the conclusion, then there is no room left for skepticism about the conclusion.[7] If one were to say that strong rather than valid arguments leave room for skepticism about the conclusion of an argument whose premises we have good reason to believe, then strong arguments are not good by that standard. So I propose the following.

The Mark of Irrationality   If someone recognizes that an argument is good, then it is irrational for him or her not to believe the conclusion is true.

This is a mark of irrationality for reasoning, one we can use, for we can inquire of someone whether he or she thinks that an argument is good and whether he or she believes the conclusion.[8]

We have a necessary condition for conscious rationality for reasoning, or simply ***rationality***. I suspect it is also sufficient. Note that if this is all there is to rationality, then we cannot say of someone that he or she is rational, but only rational with respect to a particular piece of reasoning. Someone may be said to act rationally or irrationally at this time. For a person to be "perfectly rational," he or she would always accept conclusions of arguments that they recognize as good.[9]

Still, "rational" is often used in other ways.[10]

Irrational ≠ ignorant

If someone doesn't know that some claim is true, and he can't supply it in some reasoning, that does not mean he is irrational. If we wish to tie rationality to what one *should* know, then there would be no clear standard of rationality. "But everyone knows that!" Are you sure? Just how much common knowledge is to be assumed?

Irrational ≠ poor reasoner

Can someone who does not use our logical standards be said to be irrational? As A. J. Ayer says, "A rational man is one who makes a proper use of reason."[11]

But then the intuitionist mathematician can claim that all classical mathematicians are irrational. And vice-versa.[12]

Further, few if any of us reason more than rarely according to a clearly enunciated logic. For one thing, a lot of the reasoning we do every day cannot be formalized in a logic that has clear standards.[13]

If we are to say that anyone who does not reason as we do is irrational, then all Pyrrhonian skeptics are irrational. They suspend judgment about the bases of logical systems, the claims that are needed to justify why a particular logical standard is correct/should be adopted. They, it seems to me, are not irrational. Someone who is not willing to take a claim on faith is not irrational.

Irrational ≠ stupid

But can't we say that someone who is stupid, who can't master the fundamentals of reasoning, acts irrationally?

I cannot see how to differentiate a stupid person from one who does not accept our logical standards. To the justification of intuitionistic logic, the child, the stupid person, the classical mathematician, and the Pyrrhonian skeptic will all reply, "I just don't get it."

Are dogs irrational?

By the mark of irrationality I propose, we cannot say that dogs are irrational. Dogs do not reason according to arguments, or at least we have no reason to believe that a dog ever accepts an argument as good.

So dogs have no (apparent) logical standards. They are like stupid people or Pyrrhonian skeptics. Shouldn't we classify them all as irrational?

Rationality then would be a global attribute of a person or creature: the ability to reason, not just in relation to a particular piece of reasoning.[14] Should we then accept as rational anyone who has a clear standard of reasoning, no matter how bizarre? But why not then accept as rational someone who reasons bizarrely by our standards, but who has never reflected on his or her standards of argumentation? Do only good logicians reason rationally? Or are we to say that only people who reason and behave as we do are rational, even though we don't always reason perfectly?

Best, perhaps, is to say that "rational" and "irrational" apply only to creatures who use language.[15] Dogs are not irrational; they are *arational*.[16]

Irrational ≠ crazy
Perhaps we could classify someone as irrational who does not believe his own experiences. He sees the sun rise and asks an authority if it's daytime. He asks his wife if the dog that comes to him at the door is their dog. Such a person isn't irrational; he's just crazy.

Irrational ≠ inconsistent
Can't we say that someone who consciously holds inconsistent beliefs is irrational? Certainly, but what does the word "irrational" add to our analysis of the person's beliefs? Nothing that I can see.[17]

The following principle summarizes how I believe rationality can enter into the analysis of someone's reasoning.

The Principle of Rational Discussion   We assume that the other person with whom we are deliberating or whose argument we are reading:

- Knows about the subject under discussion.
- Is able and willing to reason well.
- Is not lying.

If the person does not satisfy these conditions, he or she is not "playing by the rules," and our analysis of his or her reasoning can only serve to demonstrate that. This is the best definition of *rational discussion* I can formulate: one in which all participants satisfy this principle. We explicitly make clear that reasoning well is by *our* standards. When this principle is violated, it seems clearer to me to say that the conditions for rational discussion are not in place than to say that the other person is irrational.[18]

Conscious rationality for behavior
There is one way in which conscious belief is strongly connected to behavior. A *prescriptive claim* is one that says what someone should or should not do.[19] For example, "Dick should close the window," "You should not torture children," "No one should keep a cat as a pet." But just because you should do something, even if you believe you should do it, does not mean that you actually do it.

The Mark of Irrationality for Prescriptions A person is irrational
to believe a prescription and to act consciously in a way that he or
she knows is incompatible with it.

This, too, is a mark we can use, for we can inquire of someone
whether he or she believes a particular prescriptive claim and recognizes that he or she is acting inconsistently with it.[20]

Note that since this mark is for conscious rationality, the person
has to know that he or she is acting in a way that is incompatible with
their consciously held belief. For example, someone might believe
"You should not harm dogs" and yet give her puppy a square of
chocolate every day. Unless she is aware that chocolate is harmful
to the puppy, she is not acting irrationally.[21] Thus, this notion of
rationality depends on the notion of rationality for reasoning since
it requires of someone that he or she recognizes an inconsistency.

Dispositional rationality

This is rationality that we ascribe to others based on our observations of
them in terms of their dispositional beliefs. Those beliefs must include,
if we are to analyze them, a dispositional logic as well as dispositional
or conscious goals.[22]

Though our analysis of others' actions must assume they hold an
underlying, certainly (in part) unconscious logic in order for us to make
some sense of what they do, we need not assume the person is actually
reasoning. Indeed, if the person is reasoning, then it is conscious
rationality that is at issue.

What many discussions of dispositional rationality seem to focus
on is whether the person is consistent in his or her dispositional beliefs
(and goals) as inferred from his or her actions, and whether the person
acts consistently with his or her beliefs. I think that what is meant is
that the belief we infer from the person's most recent action is consistent with the other dispositional (and conscious) beliefs we ascribe to
him or her. I prefer to say, then, that the person *appears to be acting
inconsistently with his or her beliefs* or, for short, the person *is
apparently acting inconsistently*, since this notion of dispositional
rationality is so tenuously linked to reasoning.[23]

But typically authors say that a person acts rationally if his beliefs
are "by and large" consistent or are consistent "for the most part."[24]
This seems like saying my computer is more or less on, or an argument

is more or less valid. Consistency is absolute, there is no "more or less" to it. Perhaps what would serve here is that a particular dispositional belief is apparently consistent with the few other dispositional beliefs we are paying attention to and ascribe to the person.[25]

Some say that a person is acting irrationally when he or she does something that seems to be not in his or her best interests. That word "seems" is crucial, for it seems *to us* that he or she is not acting in his or her own best interests. But that does not mean that he or she shares our premises or our standards of reasoning. It is difficult to supply missing premises when we do not have the arguer with us to confirm our choices.[26] It is much more difficult to supply whole arguments for someone who is simply acting.

Often people speak of "apparently irrational beliefs" when they mean the beliefs apparently are not founded on good reasons. That is, *the person could not give a good argument for his or her belief.* But if that is the standard of irrationality, then almost all of us, almost all the time, would be irrational. Alternatively, we might understand it to mean that *we* cannot give a good argument for the person's belief, based on the other beliefs we attribute to him or her, which would have to include their ability to reason well. And that tells us more about our understanding of the other person than about the other person's ability to reason or hold well-founded beliefs.[27]

Conclusion

I, too, would like to label some people I know as irrational based on what they do. After all, I am quite rational, and it always surprises me how irrational others are and how often I have to say to them "Be rational: agree with me." But to differentiate that from simply labeling them "stupid" or "bad reasoner" (or just not liking what they do), I should be able to state: 1. A minimum level of knowledge, 2. The norms of reasoning that I accept, and 3. Rules for how to infer not only beliefs but what forms of reasoning a person is using based on what he or she does. That seems very hard. And in the end, the label "rational" or "irrational" seems to add no more to such an analysis than a value judgment.[28]

This is not to deny the importance of our daily attempts to understand others by ascribing beliefs to them. And often enough we have practical success. But nothing in that success requires or is made clearer by adding the label "rational."

Appendix: Irrational emotions

"Zoe has an irrational fear of spiders."

We hear comments like this all the time. What does it mean?

If "rationality" in this case has something to do with reasoning, then it must mean that Zoe doesn't have a good argument for being afraid of spiders, or at least can't recognize that she has no good argument. She just gets afraid of them whenever she sees them, however harmless they are and however easy it would be to swat them with a newspaper.

Or perhaps it means that Dick has told her patiently, time and again, that there's no good reason to be afraid of spiders. He's given good arguments against being afraid of spiders, and Zoe even recognizes that they're good, so she believes that she shouldn't be afraid of spiders. But she's still afraid of them. So, it seems, she has the Mark of Irrationality for Prescriptions.

But this is to suppose that Zoe has the ability not to be afraid of spiders. She *should* be not afraid, and with that "should" comes "is able to." [29]   Yet that is exactly what doesn't happen with Zoe: it's not under her control. She just gets afraid, wildly afraid.

Emotions are not under our control, or only loosely so for mild emotions. Perhaps we can train ourselves, with great effort, not to have a certain kind of emotion in a particular situation, like the young man who learns not to feel joy when he sees a girl he loves who rejected him because he's found it leads to unhappiness later. But strong emotions "grip us," we are "in the sway" of them, we are "carried away" with them.[30]

Zoe may have no justification for her fear of spiders. She may have seen good arguments that show spiders are no danger to her, and she even acknowledges that they are good arguments. But for this to justify our calling her "irrational" it must be that she is able not to have the emotion in those circumstances: whether to have the emotion or not has to be under the control of her reasoning abilities. And that is exactly what isn't the case.

Anyway, it's more likely that Zoe looks at Dick's argument and says it's not good: all Dick has shown is "There is very little, almost no chance of being hurt by a spider here." That little chance is enough for her, as she says, "There can never be an excess of caution in avoiding spiders." She is valuing the goal of avoiding getting hurt by spiders much more highly than Dick does. Her aims and the values she places on them have to be factored into her evaluation of "You should not be afraid of spiders."

It doesn't seem that "rational" or "irrational" as epithets concerning reasoning apply to people having emotions. At best we can say that having a strong emotion such as Zoe being afraid of spiders is not a feeling or action that Zoe can control with her reasoning. But that doesn't say much. Any time we have a strong emotion, we can't control that by reasoning. We don't reason to our emotions, we just have them. We can best describe the situation with Zoe as: Zoe is afraid of spiders, and she doesn't have any good reason to believe they are really harmful to her. Adding "irrational" to that description hardly improves it.[31]

NOTES

1. (p. 181) For example, Michael E. Bratman in *Intention, Plans, and Practical Reason* uses rationality as a key concept in his analysis of intentions and planning:

> My intention must *somehow* influence my later action; otherwise why bother today to form an intention about tomorrow? It will be suggested that, once formed, my intention today to take a United flight tomorrow will persist until tomorrow and then guide what will then be present action. But presumably such an intention is not irrevocable between today and tomorrow. Such irrevocability would clearly be irrational; after all, things change and we do not always correctly anticipate the future. But this suggests that tomorrow I should continue to take the United flight only if it would be rational of me then to form such an intention from scratch. But then why should I bother deciding today what to do tomorrow? So it seems that future-directed intentions will be (1) metaphysically objection-able (since they involve action at a distance), or (2) rationally objec-tionable (since they are irrevocable), or (3) just a waste of time. p. 5

But nothing in this passage or later in his book makes clear what notion of rationality (among the many considered in this paper) he is invoking.

2. (p. 181) See "Arguments" in this volume for a definition and discussion of the notion of claim.

Such beliefs are sometimes called "occurrent beliefs," though Ronald de Sousa in "How to Give a Piece of Your Mind: Or, the Logic of Belief and Assent" distinguishes those two notions.

3. (p. 182) Norman Malcolm in "Thoughtless Brutes" says animals have beliefs. Others disagree, and there is little consensus in this area. See Gabriel Segal "Belief (2): Epistemology" for a discussion and survey. Ronald de Sousa in "How to Give a Piece of Your Mind" says:

> In reporting someone's beliefs in indirect discourse our latitude is limited by the canons of acceptable paraphrase; but in the case of animals and infants, it is limited only by explanatory or descriptive purposes for which the ascription is made. And this is not due to the limitations on our access to the beliefs of dumb creatures, but to the fact that they do not have specific beliefs. Only sentences can specify beliefs, and a belief need not be specific at all until it has been formulated. pp. 61–62

4. (p. 182) But see Jonathan Bennett *Rationality*. Another kind of nonlinguistic belief is suggested by others who take beliefs to be abstract propositions, thoughts, or sets of possible worlds. Those are then correlated in

some manner to the thoughts of persons or things. See Michael Tye "Beliefs
(1): Metaphysics" for a summary of various views. For the discussion here it
will be enough to pay attention to linguistic correlates of those kinds of beliefs.

In "Language, Thought, and Meaning" in *Reasoning and Formal Logic*
in this series I set out a conception of thought that can apply to animals. See
also "Subjective Claims" in this volume for a discussion of attributing thought
to animals.

5. (p. 182) See Donald Davidson, "Rational Animals."

6. (p. 183) See "Arguments" in this volume for a definition and discussion
about arguments.

7. (p. 183) These are the conditions for an argument to be good that are
discussed in "Arguments" in this volume.

8. (p. 183) Compare the analysis of rationality by Robert Nozick in *The
Nature of Rationality*:

> I shall propose two rules to govern rational belief: not believing any
> statement less credible than some incompatible alternative — the
> intellectual component — but then believing a statement only if the
> expected utility (or decision-value) of doing so is greater than that
> of not believing it — the practical component. p. xiv

Even if credibility is allowed to depend on what can be arrived at through
reasoning, this is weaker than my standard: it would allow for one to suspend
judgment on the conclusion of an argument that he or she deems good. The
second part of his definition is discussed below.

Alternatively, we could take the mark of irrationality to be that someone
recognizes an argument is good but believes the conclusion is false. That
would implicitly require that it is irrational both to believe a claim and not
believe it. Since at least Aristotle this has typically been subsumed under
"It is irrational to believe both A and not-A."

One could also define a person to be *semi-irrational* if he or she recognizes that the only argument(s) he or she has for a claim are weak, yet still
believes the claim. But the person may have good motives to believe the claim
and not be able to verbalize them.

One colleague suggested that what I take to be the mark of irrationality is
meta-irrationality: first you rationally recognize an argument is good, then you
irrationally reject it. "Just plain irrationality is not recognizing that a good
argument is good in the first place." I consider that below.

9. (p. 183) Roy A. Sorensen in "Rationality as an Absolute Concept" takes
rationality to be defined in negative terms: the absence of certain kinds of
irrationalities. This is what I do in defining rationality as the lack of the mark

of irrationality, though my Principle of Rational Discussion below sets out positive criteria, too. Sorensen's notion of what vices must be avoided to be rational, however, seems similar to defining "fallacy" in terms of lists of fallacies without an underlying analysis of the concept. For example,

> An irrationality is an inefficiency in this system of rules [of thinking]—a bad belief policy. We achieve the goal of getting true beliefs and avoiding false ones by accumulating and processing information. Although a rational man's hunger for new information is limited by its costs, he does gobble up cheap relevant information. A worried picnicker who refuses to check the weather report is irrational because he is giving up a golden opportunity to get germane news. p. 476

I think that it is better to label such a picnicker "willfully ignorant" rather than "irrational."

10. (p. 183) What follows is not meant to be an exhaustive list of views of rationality. For example, John Kekes, "Rationality and Problem Solving," p. 266, says that theories are rational or irrational:

> A theory is rational if it provides a possible solution to the problem the theory was meant to solve, and it is irrational if it fails to do so.

Kekes is discussing something interesting, but not, it seems to me, rationality. For a survey on rationality, especially in relation to relativism and the possibility of translation, see Stanley Jeyaraja Tambiah, *Magic, Science, Religion, and the Scope of Rationality*, especially Chapter 6, and Martin Hollis and Stephen Lukes, *Rationality and Relativism*.

11. (p. 184) *Probability and Evidence.* The quote continues, "and this implies, among other things, that he correctly estimates the strength of evidence."

12. (p. 184) See Carnielli's and my *Computability* for a comparison of the views of intuitionist and constructivist mathematicians versus classical mathematicians.

13. (p. 184) See my "The World as Process" and the essays in *Cause and Effect, Conditionals, Explanations*.

14. (p. 184) Donald Davidson, "Incoherence and Irrationality," believes that there are some universal standards of reasoning by which anyone could be judged, objectively, to be irrational:

> It does not make sense to ask, concerning a creature with propositional attitudes, whether that creature is *in general* rational, whether its attitudes and intentional actions are in accord with the basic standards of rationality. Rationality, in this primitive sense, is a condition of having thoughts at all. The question whether the creature "subscribes"

to the principle of continence, or to the logic of the sentential calculus, or to the principle of total evidence for inductive reasoning, is not an empirical question. For it is only by interpreting a creature as largely in accord with these principles that we can intelligibly attribute propositional attitudes to it, or that we can raise the question whether it is in some respect irrational. We see then that my word "subscribe" is misleading. Agents can't *decide* whether or not to accept the fundamental attributes of rationality: if they are in a position to decide anything, they have those attributes. p. 352

Davidson invokes a Kantian precondition for thought. But he invokes no evidence that ordinary people or even logicians actually use these principles in their daily reasoning, no linguistic or anthropological studies. Indeed, many have rejected classical logic, which Davidson apparently intends; see "Why Are There So Many Logics?" in *Reasoning and Formal Logic* in this series, though I suggest there that there may be some forms of propositional reasoning that underlie all propositional logics. And the principle of total evidence that Rudolf Carnap presents in *Logical Foundations of Probability*, p. 211, is impossible to apply in reasoning in ordinary life. Davidson's views can better be defended as declaring a standard of irrationality relative to a particular community of reasoners, as in my Principle of Rational Discussion below.

Jonathan Bennett in *Rationality* says

I use 'rationality' to mean 'whatever it is that humans possess which marks them off, in respect of intellectual capacity, sharply and importantly from all other known species'. p. 5

Bennett then, without explanation, restricts his attention to human reasoning abilities (p. 10) and finally characterizes rationality:

The expression of dated and universal judgments is both necessary and sufficient for rationality, and thus linguistic capacity is necessary but not sufficient for rationality. p. 94

However, his examples and comments throughout make it clear that he takes as the archetype of rationality the empiricist who uses the scientific method.

15. (p. 185) De Sousa in "Rational Animals: What the Bravest Lion Won't Risk" says:

The crucial threshold [for determining rationality] that animals do not cross consists in our capacity to be *irrational*. And in turn, the capacity to be irrational rests on our capacity *to speak*.

See also Jonathan Bennett, *Rationality*.

16. (p. 185) Luciano Floridi in "Scepticism and Animal Rationality" presents a history of views of the rationality of dogs which illuminates much of the discussion here.

The papers in Susan Hurley and Matthew Nudds' *Rational Animals?* discuss animal rationality principally in terms of behavioral rationality discussed below.

17. (p. 185) Frank P. Ramsey in *The Foundation of Mathematics and Other Logical Essays* and others take consistency in a very strong form as the criterion of rationality: the person must be an idealized gambler. But as I point out in "Probabilities" in this volume, this seems much too strong a standard, certainly much stronger than the Principle of Rational Discussion below.

Somewhat weaker is the use of probability to legislate rationality proposed by Henry E. Kyburg, Jr. in "The Nature of Epistemological Probability":

> The epistemological import of probability is that it is *legislative* for rational belief: if K is the set of statements corresponding to my body of knowledge, my degree of belief in a statement S *should* reflect the probability of S relative to K. p. 153

But this makes rationality dependent on a notion that is not essential for reasoning, as I discuss in "Probabilities" in this volume.

18. (p. 185) See "Arguments" in this volume for a fuller discussion.

19. (p. 186) See "Reasoning with Prescriptive Claims" in *Prescriptive Reasoning*.

20. (p. 186) This notion of rationality depends on understanding what it means to say that a way of acting is inconsistent with a particular prescriptive claim. Roughly, that can be explained by saying that a claim that describes that way of acting is inconsistent with a claim that describes the world in which the prescription is done. For example, "Dick should take the trash out after dinner" and "Dick went to bed directly after dinner" are incompatible since the latter is inconsistent with "Dick takes the trash out after dinner." See "Reasoning with Prescriptive Claims" in *Prescriptive Reasoning*.

21. (p. 186) Chocolate is toxic to dogs and can lead to death—unfortunately of the dog.

22. (p. 186) See, for example, Chapter 5 of Gilbert Ryle, *The Concept of Mind*. Compare also Davidson, "Rational Animals." See also "Reasoning with Prescriptive Claims" in this volume.

23. (p. 187) Charles Taylor in "Rationality" says:

> What do we mean by rationality? We often tend to reach for a characterization in formal terms. Rationality can be seen as logical consistency, for instance. We can call someone irrational who affirms both p and not-p. By extension, someone who acts flagrantly in violation of his own interests, or of his own avowed objectives, can be considered irrational.

This can be seen as a possible extension of the case of logical inconsistency, because we are imputing to this agent end E, and we throw in the principle: who wills the end wills the means. And then we see him acting to prevent means M from eventuating, acting as it were on the maxim: let me prevent M. Once you spell it out, this makes a formal inconsistency.

Can we then understand the irrationality in terms of the notion of inconsistency? It might appear so for the following reason: the mere fact of having E as an end and acting to prevent M isn't sufficient to convict the agent of irrationality. He might not realize that the correct description of his end was 'E'; he might not know that M was the indispensable means; he might not know that what he was now doing was incompatible with M. In short, he has to know, in some sense, that he is frustrating his own goals, before we are ready to call him irrational. Of course, the knowledge we attribute to him may be of a rather special kind. He may be unable or unwilling to acknowledge the contradiction; but in this case, our imputation of irrationality depends on our attributing unconscious knowledge to him.

Thus logical inconsistency may seem the core of our concept of irrationality, because we think of the person who acts irrationally as having the wherewithal to formulate the maxims of his action and objectives which are in contradiction with each other.

Possibly inconsistency is enough to explain the accusations of irrationality that we bandy around in our civilization. But our concept of rationality is richer. And this we can see when we consider . . . are there standards of rationality that are valid across cultures? p. 87

Taylor then devotes the rest of his paper to this last topic. What seems interesting in the cases he cites are the reasons we give for calling members of another culture (Azande or 17th century opponents of Galileo) irrational: they don't know what we know; they don't understand the world as we do; they don't reason as we do; they don't want to reason as we do; . . . . Calling them "irrational" doesn't add anything to that analysis and doesn't seem to sum up such analyses in any useful way, but rather clouds what we have learned about people of those cultures with what amounts to a value judgment. In the end, Taylor comes close to the notion of (conscious) rationality that I propose:

But incommensurable ways of life seem to raise the question insistently of who is right. It's hard to avoid this, since anyone seriously practising magic in our society would be considered to have lost his grip on reality, and if he continued impervious to counter-arguments, he would be thought less than fully rational. p. 100

Being impervious to counter-arguments amounts to either an inability or unwillingness to reason well (by our standards) or to possessing the mark of irrationality. Compare S. L. Zabell, "Ramsey, Truth, and Probability":

> It is the credibilist view of probability that if you knew what I knew, and I knew what you knew, then you and I would—or at least should—agree. . . . It is an article of faith of no real practical importance. None of us can grasp the totality of our own past history, experience, and information, let alone anyone else's. The goal is impossible: our information cannot be so encapsulated. But we *would* regard a person as irrational if we could not convert him to our viewpoint, no matter *how much* evidence he was provided with. From this perspective, irrationality is the *persistence* in a viewpoint in the face of mounting and cumulative evidence to the contrary.   p. 232

24. (p. 187) Jon Elster in *Sour Grapes: Studies in the Subversion of Rationality*:

> The process of belief imputation must be guided by the assumption that they [beliefs of a person] are by and large consistent. p. 4

25. (p. 187) An alternative might be to base our reasoning on a paraconsistent logic, that is, a logic that tolerates local inconsistencies. But even in paraconsistent logics, as I have shown in a few cases in *Propositional Logics*, consistency can be understood as global and 2-valued, as in classical logic.

Dan Sperber in "Apparently Rational Beliefs" wants to attribute rationality to beliefs:

> A proposition can be paradoxical, counter-intuitive or self-contradictory, but, in and by itself, it cannot be irrational. What can be rational or irrational is what one does with a proposition, for instance asserting it, denying it, entertaining it, using it as a premise in a logical derivation, etc. Thus to decide whether some belief is rational we need to know not only its content but also in which sense it is 'believed'. p. 164

> How exactly 'belief' should be defined is for psychologists to discover. But even without a full characterization, some of the necessary conditions for a belief to be rational can be specified. A belief is not rational unless it is self-consistent and consistent with other beliefs held simultaneously. p. 165

But why should we pick out one and not another belief to label as "irrational" from a collection that is not consistent? Donald Davidson in "Incoherence and Irrationality", p. 348, gives a reason which I find too vague:

> No factual belief *by itself*, no matter how egregious it seems to others, can be held to be irrational. It is only when beliefs are inconsistent with other beliefs according to principles held by the

agent himself—in other words, only when there is an inner inconsistency—that there is a clear case of irrationality. . . .

We often do say of a single belief or action or emotion that it is irrational, but I think on reflection it will be found that this is because we assume in these cases that there must be an inner inconsistency. The item we choose to call irrational is apt then to be the one by rejecting which things are most economically brought back into line.

26. (p. 187) Hundreds of examples in *Critical Thinking* illustrate this.

Richard Feldman in "Rationality, Reliability, and Natural Selection" shows that the examples given by Stephen Stich of attributing irrationality to animals or people by interpreting their actions are not convincing because there are so many other ways to interpret their actions according to better inferences—if, as he notes, the animals (rats, toads) really have any beliefs.

27. (p. 187) For the relation of rationality as the ability to reason vs. rationality as the ability to make decisions, with many references especially to the literature in psychology, see J. St. B. T. Evans, D. E. Over, and K. I. Manktelow, "Reasoning, Decision Making and Rationality." The problem that pervades the writing of psychologists on rationality is that in claiming someone is reasoning badly they offer no explicit standards or at least no justification of what constitutes good reasoning; as an example, see Thomas Gilovich, *How We Know What Isn't So.* Or worse, the psychologists' standards of reasoning are wrong; for instance, J. St. B. T. Evans and D. E. Over say in *Rationality and Reasoning*:

> In syllogist reasoning tasks, subjects are presented with two premises and a conclusion. They are instructed to say whether the conclusion follows logically from the premises. They are told that a valid conclusion is one that must be true if the premises are true and that nothing other than the premises is relevant to this judgement. p. 3

They have misstated the criterion of validity, which is: it must be that if the premises are true, the conclusion is true. A subject might take their criterion at face value and classify an argument as invalid if its conclusion isn't necessary.

Stephen Nathanson in *The Ideal of Rationality* relies completely on external evaluations of actions:

> Deliberation is not a necessary condition of a rational action. For example, it can be rational for me to stop at the curb of a busy street prior to crossing even though I have not evaluated this action with respect to my goals, assessed its efficacy as a means, made unbiased and objective judgments, and so on. While this kind of evaluation would yield the conclusion that my action is rational, I need not consciously carry out the evaluation myself in order for my stopping to be rational. The probable results of my stopping or not stopping

are the measure of the rationality of my action, and no reference is required to a method criterion of rationality.   p. 39

By this standard my dogs are acting rationally all the time. Or at least it seems so to me as I try to interpret the "probable results" of their actions.

Christopher Cherniak in *Minimal Rationality* also looks to actions as the key to rationality. He wishes to lower the standard of what is rational from an ideal reasoner to one who fulfills what he calls the *minimal general rationality condition*:

> If *A* has a particular belief set, *A* would undertake some, but not necessarily all, of those actions that are apparently appropriate.

This criterion would have the consequence that a lot more people, perhaps everyone, would be classified as rational, if we could decide how to apply it.

See also Carl G. Hempel, "Aspects of Scientific Explanation", section 10, for his account of rationality in these terms and the nature of explanations.

Susan Hurley and Matthew Nudds discuss three different notions of rationality in "The Questions of Animal Rationality: Theory and Evidence," pp. 21–22 (italics in original):

> *PP-rationality* is typically adopted by philosophers and cognitive psychologists. On this conception, rationality is exhibited when beliefs or actions are adopted on the basis of appropriate reasons. PP-rationality focuses on the process by which belief or action is arrived at, rather than the outcome of beliefs or actions.

> There is a conception of rationality prevalent in economics according to which behaviour that maximizes expected utility is rational, no matter how it was produced or selected; Kacelnik calls this *E-rationality*.

> A *B-rational* individual is one whose behaviour maximizes its inclusive fitness across a set of evolutionary relevant circumstances. In its emphasis on outcomes rather than processes and on consistency B-rationality is similar to E-rationality. B-rationality entails E-rationality in relevant circumstances, but goes beyond it to specify that *what* is maximized must be inclusive fitness.

See "Models and Theories" in *Reasoning in Science and Mathematics* in this series for a critique of the notion of rationality in economics.

28. (p. 188) Compare the view described by John Heil in "Belief":

> A different anti-realist tack is taken by Daniel Dennett, who defends an 'instrumentalist' conception of belief. We have a practical interest in regarding certain 'systems' — people, animals, machines, even committees — as rational, as registering, on the whole, what is true

and as reasoning in accord with appropriate norms. In so doing, we take up an 'intentionalist stance'. We are, as a result, in a position to make sense of and, within limits, to predict the behaviour of the systems in question. The practical success of this enterprise, however, does not depend on its yielding true descriptions of states and goings-on inside agents.

Allan Gibbard in *Wise Choices, Apt Feelings* says he wants to stay close to the ordinary language use of "rational":

> The rational act is what it makes sense to do, the right choice on the occasion. A rational feeling is an apt feeling, a warranted feeling, a way it makes sense to feel about something. The term 'rational' may carry narrower suggestions, but this broad, endorsing reading is the one I need. . . .
>
> . . . To call something rational is to express one's acceptance of norms that permit it. This formula applies to almost anything that can be appraised as rational or irrational—persons aside. It applies to the rationality of actions, and it applies to the rationality of beliefs and feelings. We assess a wide range of things as rational or irrational, and it is puzzling how this can be. The analysis offers an answer. p. 7

A better answer is that we are implicitly attributing rationality to the actor and not to the belief or feeling. To extend the notion of rationality so far is to end up with a word that isn't going to illuminate our discussions.

29. (p. 189) See "Reasoning with Prescriptive Claims" in *Prescriptive Reasoning* for conditions for a should-claim to be true.

30. (p. 189) See "The Directedness of Emotions" in *Cause and Effect, Conditionals, Explanations* for a fuller discussion of this.

31. (p. 190) Amélie O. Rorty in "Explaining Emotions" says:

> A person's emotion is irrational if correcting the belief presupposed by the emotion fails to change it appropriately *or* if the person uncharacteristically resists considerations that would normally lead him to correct the belief. But an emotion can be irrational even if the presupposed belief is true; for the true belief presupposed by the emotion need not be its cause, even when the person does genuinely hold it. The emotion may be caused by beliefs or attitudes that bear no relation to the belief that would rationalize it, quite independently of whether the person does in fact also have the rationalizing belief. The rationality or irrationality of an emotion is a function of the relation between its causes and the beliefs that are taken to justify it. But irrational emotions can sometimes be perfectly appropriate to the situation in which they occur; and an emotion can be inappropriate

when there is no irrationality (if, for instance, it is too strong or too weak, out of balance with other emotions that are appropriate). Both judgments of rationality and of appropriateness involve conceptions of normality that have normative force. Disagreements about the classification of an emotion often disguise disagreements about what is wholesome or right. p. 123

But what is a belief presupposed by an emotion? Presupposed by whom? See "The Directedness of Emotions" in *Cause and Effect, Conditionals, Explanations* in this series where that issue is discussed in the context of trying to clarify the distinction between a cause and an object of an emotion. I think Rorty has it right in her last sentence: it isn't rationality that is at issue with emotions, but whether an emotion is right, or wholesome, or prevents the fulfillment of other aims the person holds as highly.

Bibliography

Page references are to the most recent publication cited unless noted otherwise.
Italics in quotations are in the original source.

ARISTOTLE
  1941 *The Basic Works of Aristotle*
        Ed. Richard McKeon, Random House. This includes:
            Analytica Priora (selections) Trans. A. J. Jenkinson.
            De Sophisticis Elenchis (selections) Trans. E. M. Edghill.
AYER, A. J.
  1972 *Probability and Evidence: An Analysis of the Foundations and
        Structure of Knowledge*
        Colombia University Press.
AUDI, Robert, ed.
  1995 *The Cambridge Dictionary of Philosophy*
        Cambridge University Press.
BACON, Francis
  1620 *Novum Organum*
        ed. Joseph Devey, P. F. Collier, 1902.
BENNETT, Jonathan
  1964 *Rationality: An Essay Towards an Analysis*
        Routledge. Reprinted 1989 with a new preface, Hackett.
BERG, Jonathan
  1987 Interpreting Arguments
        Informal Logic IX.1, pp. 13–21.
BLACK, Max
  1967 Induction
        In EDWARDS vol. 4, pp. 169–181.
  1967 Probability
        In EDWARDS vol. 6, pp. 464–479.
BOLZANO, Bernard
  1837 *Theory of Science.*
        Translation by Rolf George of *Wissenschaftslehre,*
        University of California Press, 1972.
BRATMAN, Michael
  1987 *Intention, Plans, and Practical Reason*
        Harvard University Press.
BRUX, Jacqueline Murray and Janna L. COWAN
  2002 *Economic Issues and Policy*
        Southwestern.

BURKE, Michael B.
   1994   Denying the Antecedent: A Common Fallacy?
           Informal Logic, XVI, pp. 23–30.

CAHN, Steven M.
   1967   *Fate, Logic, and Time*
           Yale University Press.

CARNAP, Rudolf
   1950   *Logical Foundations of Probability*
           University of Chicago Press.

CARROLL, Lewis
   1895   What the Tortoise Said to Achilles
           Mind, n.s. 4, pp. 278–280.

CEDERBLOM, Jerry and David W. PAULSEN
   1996   *Critical Reasoning*
           4th ed., Wadsworth.

CHAKRABARTI, Kisor Kumar
   1995   *Definition and Induction: A Historical and Comparative Study*
           University of Hawai'i Press.

CHENEY, Dorothy L. and Robert M. SEYFARTH
   2007   *Baboon Metaphysics: The Evolution of a Social Mind*
           University of Chicago Press.

CHERNIAK, Christopher
   1986   *Minimal Rationality*
           MIT Press.

COHEN, L. Jonathan
   1989   *An Introduction to the Philosophy of Induction and Probability*
           Clarendon Press, Oxford.

COPI, Irving M.
   1972   *Introduction to Logic*
           4th edition, Macmillan.

DAMER, T. Edward
   1995   *Attacking Faulty Reasoning*
           3rd ed., Wadsworth.

DAVIDSON, Donald
   1982   Rational Animals
           Dialectica, vol. 36, pp. 318–327.
   1985   Incoherence and Irrationality
           Dialectica, vol. 39, pp. 345–354.

DE FINETTI, Bruno
   1931   Sul Significato Soggettivo della Probabilità
           Fundamenta Mathematicae, vol. XVII, pp. 298–329.
   1964   Foresight: Its Logical Laws, Its Subjective Sources

In *Studies in Subjective Probability,* eds. H. E. Kyburg and H. E. Smokler, John Wiley & Sons, Inc., pp. 93–158. A translation and revision of *La Prévision: Ses Lois Logiques, Ses Sources Subjectives,* Annales de L'Institut Henri Poincaré, vol. 7, pp. 1–68.

DENNETT, Daniel
　1987　*The Intentional Stance*
　　　　MIT Press.

DE SOUSA, Ronald
　1971　How to Give a Piece of Your Mind: Or, the Logic of Belief and Assent
　　　　Review of Metaphysics, XXV, pp. 52–79.
　2002　Twelve Varieties of Subjectivity: Dividing in Hopes of Conquest
　　　　In *Knowledge, Language, and Representation*, eds. J. M.
　　　　Larrazabal and L. A. Pérez Miranda, Kluwer.
　2004　Rational Animals: What the Bravest Lion Won't Risk
　　　　Croatian Journal of Philosophy IV-2, pp. 365–386.

EDWARDS, Paul, ed.
　1967　*The Encyclopedia of Philosophy,*
　　　　The Free Press.

ELSTER, Jon
　1983　*Sour Grapes: Studies in the Subversion of Rationality*
　　　　Cambridge University Press.

EPSTEIN, Richard L.
　1990　*Propositional Logics*
　　　　Kluwer. 3rd edition, Advanced Reasoning Forum, 2012.
　1994　*Predicate Logic*
　　　　Oxford University Press. Advanced Reasoning Forum, 2012.
　1998　*Critical Thinking*
　　　　4th edition with Michael Rooney, Advanced Reasoning Forum, 2013.
　2001　*Five Ways of Saying "Therefore"*
　　　　Wadsworth.
　2012　The World as Process
　　　　To appear in *Reasoning and Formal Logic*.

EPSTEIN, Richard L. and Walter A. CARNIELLI
　1989　*Computability*
　　　　Wadsworth. 3rd ed., Advanced Reasoning Forum, 2008.

EPSTEIN, Richard L. and Stanislaw KRAJEWSKI
　2004　Relatedness predicate logic
　　　　Bulletin of Advanced Reasoning and Knowledge, vol. 2,
　　　　2004, pp. 19–38. At www.AdvancedReasoningForum.org.

EVANS, J. St. B. T. and D. E. OVER
　1996　*Rationality and Reasoning*
　　　　Psychology Press.

EVANS, J. St. B. T. and D. E. OVER and K. I. MANKTELOW
    1993   Reasoning, Decision Making and Rationality
           Cognition, vol. 49, pp. 165–187.

FELDMAN, Richard
    1988   Rationality, Reliability, and Natural Selection
           Philosophy of Science, vol. 55, pp. 218–277.
    1999   *Reason and Argument*
           Prentice Hall, 2nd ed.

FINOCCHIARO, Maurice
    1981   Fallacies and the Evaluation of Reasoning
           American Philosophical Quarterly, Vol. 18, pp. 13–22.
    1994   The Positive Versus the Negative Evaluation of Arguments.
           In *New Essays in Informal Logic,* eds. Ralph H. Johnson and
           J. Anthony Blair, Informal Logic, Windsor, Canada.

FLORIDI, Luciano
    1997   Scepticism and Animal Rationality
           Archiv für Geschichte der Philosophie 79, 27-57.

FOLEY, Richard
    1995   Subjectivism
           In AUDI, p. 773.

GALAVOTTI, Maria Carla
    1991   The Notion of Subjective Probability in the Work of Ramsey and
           de Finetti
           Theoria, vol. LVII, pp. 239–259.

GAUKER, Christopher
    1986   The Principle of Charity
           Synthese, 69, pp. 1–25.

GIBBARD, Allan
    1990   *Wise Choices, Apt Feelings: A Theory of Normative Judgment*
           Harvard University Press.

GILLON, Brendan
    2011   Logic in Classical Indian Philosophy
           Stanford Encyclopedia of Philosophy, http://plato.stanford.edu .

GILOVICH, Thomas
    1993   *How We Know What Isn't So*
           Free Press.

GOODMAN, Nelson
    1983   *Fact, Fiction, and Forecast*
           4th edition, Harvard University Press.

GOULD, James A.
    1998   *Classical Philosophical Questions*
           Prentice Hall.

GOVIER, Trudy
  1987 *Problems in Argument Analysis and Evaluation*
        Foris Publications. Including:
          A New Approach to Charity, pp. 133–158.
          Is a Theory of Argument Possible?, pp. 13–36.
          Two Unreceived Views about Reasoning and Argument,
            pp. 55–80.
GUTTENPLAN, S., ed.
  1994 *A Companion to the Philosophy of Mind*
        Blackwell.
HACKING, Ian
  1975 *The Emergence of Probability*
        Cambridge University Press.
HAILPERIN, Theodore
  1996 *Sentential Probability Logic*
        Lehigh University Press/Associated University Presses.
HAMBLIN, C. L.
  1970 *Fallacies*
        Methuen & Co.
HARROD, Roy
  1956 *Foundations of Inductive Logic*
        Macmillan.
HEIL, John
  1992 Belief
        In *A Companion to Epistemology*, eds. Jonathan Dancy and Ernest
        Sosa, Blackwell, pp. , pp. 45–48.
HEMPEL, Carl G.
  1943 A Purely Syntactical Definition of Confirmation
        Journal of Symbolic Logic, vol. 8, pp. 122–143.
  1965 Studies in the Logic of Confirmation
        Chapter 1 of Hempel, *Aspects of Scientific Explanation*, The Free
        Press. This is a version of an article of the same name in *Mind,*
        vol. 54, pp. 1–26 and 97–121, 1945.
  1965 Aspects of Scientific Explanation
        Chapter 12 of Hempel, 1965A.
HOLLIS, Martin and Stephen LUKES, eds.
  1982 *Rationality and Relativism*
        The MIT Press.
HUME, David
  1739 *A Treatise of Human Nature*
        Edition 1888, ed. L. A. Selby-Bigge, Oxford University Press.

HURLEY, Patrick J.
> 1997   *A Concise Introduction to Logic*
>   6th ed., Wadsworth.

HURLEY, Susan and Matthew NUDDS
> 2006   The Questions of Animal Rationality: Theory and Evidence
>   In Hurley and Nudds, eds., *Rational Animals?*, Oxford University
>   Press, pp. 1–83.

HYSLOP, Alec
> 2009   Other Minds
>   Stanford Encyclopedia of Philosophy, http://plato.stanford.edu .

JOAD, C. E. M.
> 1936   *Guide to Philosophy*
>   Victor Gollancz, Ltd. Reprinted by Dover Publications, 1957.

JOHNSON, Ralph
> 1987   The Blaze of Her Splendors
>   *Argumentation,* 1, pp. 239–253.

KAHANE, Howard
> 1995   *Logic and Contemporary Rhetoric*
>   7th edition, Wadsworth.

KEKES, John
> 1977   Rationality and Problem Solving
>   *Philosophy of the Social Sciences,* vol. 7, pp. 351–366. Reprinted in
>   J. Agassi and I. C. Jarvie, *Rationality: The Critical View*, Martinus
>   Nijhoff Publishers, 1987, pp. 265–279.

KELLEY, David.
> 1988   *The Art of Reasoning*
>   W.W. Norton & Company.

KEYNES, John Maynard
> 1921   *A Treatise on Probability*
>   Macmillan & Co.

KNEALE, William
> 1949   *Probability and Induction*
>   Clarendon Press, Oxford.

KYBURG, Henry E. Jr.
> 1966   Probability and Decision
>   *Philosophy of Science*, vol. 33, pp. 250–261. Reprinted in
>   KYBURG, 1983A, pp. 49–62.

> 1983   The Nature of Epistemological Probability
>   In KYBURG, 1983A, pp. 153–157.

> 1983A *Epistemology and Inference*
>   University of Minnesota Press.

LENZ, John W.
  1974   Problems for the Practicalist's Justification of Induction
         In *The Justification of Induction,* ed. R. Swinburne, Oxford
         University Press.
LEVI, Edward H.
  1949   *An Introduction to Legal Reasoning*
         University of Chicago Press.
LUKES, Stephen
  1982   Relativism in its Place
         HOLLIS and LUKES, pp. 261–305.
MACKIE, J. L.
  1973   *Truth, Probability, and Paradox*
         Oxford University Press.
MALCOLM, Norman
  1972   Thoughtless Brutes
         Proceedings American Philosophical Association, vol. 46, pp. 5–19.
MATES, Benson
  1996   *The Skeptic Way: Sextus Empiricus' Outlines of Pyrrhonism*
         Cambridge University Press.
MILL, John Stuart
  1874   *A System of Logic, ratiocinative and inductive, being a connected
         view of the principles of evidence and the methods of scientific
         investigation*
         8th edition, Harper & Brothers Publishers (New York).
MILLER, David
  1994   *Critical Rationalism*
         Open Court.
MOORE, Brooke Noel and Richard PARKER
  1995   *Critical Thinking*
         4th edition, Mayfield Publishing.
NAGEL, Thomas
  1974   What Is It Like to Be a Bat?
         The Philosophical Review, vol. 83, pp. 435–450.
NATHANSON, Stephen
  1985   *The Ideal of Rationality*
         Humanities Press International, Inc.
NEIDORF, Robert
  1967   *Deductive Forms*
         Harper and Row.
NIELSEN, KAI
  1967   Ethics, Problems of
         In EDWARDS, vol. 3, p. 117.

NOZICK, Robert
   1993   *The Nature of Rationality*
           Princeton University Press.
PEIRCE, Charles Sanders
   1960   A Theory of Probable Inference
           In Peirce, *Collected Papers*, eds. Charles Hartshorne and Paul
           Weiss, vol. 6.408, The Belknap Press, Harvard.
PLANTINGA, Alvin
   1981   Is Belief in God Properly Basic?
           Noûs, vol. 15, pp. 41–51.
POPPER, Karl R.
   1971   Conjectural Knowledge: My Solution to the Problem of Induction
           Revue internationale de Philosophie, 25 année, no. 95–96, fasc. 1–2.
           Reprinted as Chapter 1 of Popper, *Objective Knowledge*, Oxford
           University Press, 1972.
   1972A   *The Logic of Scientific Discovery*
           Hutchison of London.
PUTNAM, Hilary
   1967   The 'Corroboration of Theories'
           In *The Philosophy of Karl Popper,* ed. Paul A. Schilpp, Open Court
           Publishing Company, pp. 221–240.
RACHELS, James
   2000   Naturalism
           In Hugh LaFollete ed., *The Blackwell Guide to Ethical Theory*
           Blackwell, pp. 74–91.
RAMSEY, Frank P.
   1931   *The Foundations of Mathematics and Other Logical Essays*
           ed. by R. B. Braithwaite, Routledge and Kegan Paul.
REICHENBACH, Hans
   1938   *Experience and Prediction*
           University of Chicago Press.
RESCHER, Nicholas
   1980   *Induction*
           University of Pittsburgh Press.
ROBINSON, William S.
   1986   Ascription, Intentionality and Understanding
           The Monist vol. 69, pp. 584-97.
   1988   *Brains and People: An Essay on Mentality and its Causal Conditions*
           Temple University Press.
   1997   Some Nonhuman Animals Can Have Pains in a Morally
           Relevant Sense
           Biology and Philosophy, vol. 12, pp. 51–71.

2010 *Your Brain and You: What Neuroscience Means for Us*
      Goshawk Books.

RORTY, Amélie Oksenberg
  1980 Explaining Emotions
        In *Explaining Emotions*, ed. A. O. Rorty, University of California
        Press, pp. 103–126.

RUSSELL, Bertrand
  1925 *Mysticism and Logic*
        Longmans, Green, and Co.
  1948 *Human Knowledge, Its Scope and Limits*
        George Allen and Unwin.

RYLE, Gilbert
  1949 *The Concept of Mind*
        Hutchinson.

SAVAGE, L. J.
  1954 *The Foundations of Statistics*
        John Wiley & Sons, Inc.

SEGAL, Gabriel
  1994 Belief (2): Epistemology
        In GUTTENPLAN.

SHER, Gila
  1991 *The Bounds of Logic*
        The MIT Press.

SKYRMS, Brian
  1986 *Choice & Chance*
        Third edition. Wadsworth Publishing Company.
  1995 Induction
        In AUDI, pp. 368–369.

SMITH, Adam
  1776 *The Wealth of Nations*
        London

SOBER, Elliott
  1993 Epistemology for Empiricists
        Midwest Studies in Philosophy, XVIII, pp. 39–61.

SORENSEN, Roy
  1991 Rationality as an Absolute Concept
        Philosophy, vol. 66, pp. 473–486.

SPERBER, Dan
  1982 Apparently Rational Beliefs
        In HOLLIS and LUKES, pp. 149–180.

STALKER, Douglas, ed.
    1994   *Grue! The New Riddle of Induction*
            Open Court.
STRAWSON, P. F.
    1952   *Introduction to Logical Theory*
            Methuen & Co Ltd. Reprinted 1977.
TAMBIAH, Stanley Jeyaraja
    1990   *Magic, Science, Religion, and the Scope of Rationality*
            Cambridge University Press.
TAYLOR, Charles
    1982   Rationality
            In HOLLIS AND LUKES, pp. 87–105.
THOMAS, Stephen Naylor
    1986   *Practical Reasoning in Natural Language*
            3rd ed., Prentice Hall.
TYE, Michael
    1994   Beliefs (1): Metaphysics
            In GUTTENPLAN.
VAN EEMEREN, Frans H. and Rob GROOTENDORST
    1992   *Argumentation, Communication, and Fallacies*:
            A Pragma-Dialectical Perspective
            Lawrence Erlbaum Associates, Hove and London.
    1995   The Pragma-Dialectical Approach to Fallacies
            In Hans V. Hansen and Robert C. Pinto, eds., *Fallacies: Classical
            and Contemporary Readings*, Penn. State Univ. Press, pp. 130–144.
VON WRIGHT, Georg Henrik
    1960   *A Treatise on Induction and Probability*
            Littlefield, Adams & Co.
WELLMAN, Carl
    1971   *Challenge and Response: Justification in Ethics*
            Southern Illinois University Press.
WILLIAMS, Donald C.
    1947   *The Ground of Induction*
            Harvard University Press. Reissued 1963 by Russell & Russell, Inc.
WITTGENSTEIN, Ludwig
    1958   *Philosophical Investigations: The English Text of the Third Edition*
            Macmillan Publishing Co., Inc., translated by G. E. M. Anscombe.
    1969   *On Certainty*
            ed. G.E.M. Anscombe and G.H. von Wright, Harper & Row.
ZABELL, S. L.
    1991   Ramsey, Truth, and Probability
            Theoria, vol. LVII, pp. 210–238.

Index

CPSIA information can be obtained at www.ICGtesting.com
Printed in the USA
LVOW102355100213

319508LV00001B/1/P